THE 80s ANNUAL

VOL II

by
SARAH LEWIS

First Edition
Published 2017

Interior and cover design by Natalie Owen

Red Rain

ISBN: 978-1- 9998640-0- 2

THE 80s ANNUAL VOL II

by
SARAH LEWIS

20 questions with David Ball

Having met at Leeds Polytechnic in the late Seventies, David Ball and Marc Almond went on to form one of the most successful duos of the Eighties, Soft Cell. The pair's chart-topping debut single 'Tainted Love' in August 1981 was followed by a hit singles such as 'Bedsitter', 'Say Hello Wave Goodbye' and 'Torch', and albums including 'Non-Stop Erotic Cabaret' and 'Non-Stop Ecstatic Dancing'.

Following the break-up of Soft Cell in 1984, multi-instrumentalist and producer Ball has been involved in numerous music collaborations, including playing as one half of The Grid and re-mixing 'Hallo Spaceboy' for David Bowie, but still found time to answer these questions.

What is your favourite 80's song?
'Controversy' by Prince.

What was your favourite subject at school?
Art.

What job would you have done if you hadn't been a musician?
Artist.

Who was your teenage crush?
Pan's People from TOTP.

What was your worst fashion mistake of the 80s?
Having a mullet.

What was your first car?
I don't drive.

What was the first gig you ever went to?
Status Quo, Blackpool Opera House, 1972.

Where did you play your first gig?
Leeds Polytechnic, 1979.

Where is the best place you have ever visited?
New York.

What is at the top of your bucket list?
I don't have a bucket.

Which five people, living or dead, would be your ideal dinner guests?
Andy Warhol, Marilyn Monroe, Iggy Pop, Madonna, Jimi Hendrix.

Which pet hate would you consign to Room 101?
Plastic packaging that's impossible to open.

What makes you angry?
Stupid people.

What was the last film you watched?
Straight Outta Compton.

Who would play you in the film of your life?
Robert de Niro.

What are you most proud of?
My synthesizers.

What would be your perfect day?
A good day in the studio.

What is the best Christmas present you have ever had?
A reel to reel tape recorder.

And the worst?
A bright yellow 100% viscose tie bought by my Grandma when I was 13.

What are your hopes for the future?
To live as long as I'm allowed and see world peace.

Me with David in 2016

LYRICALLY CHALLENGED

Do you know every 80's song word-for-word or do you mumble made-up lines to the bits you don't know? See how many of these lyrics you can identify.
(Answers at back of book)

1 Face to face with their own disillusions,

The scars of old romances still on their cheeks.

2
Stay with me, baby, lay with me maybe, Honey, don't leave me alone.

3 Who needs to go to work to hustle for another dollar?

I'd rather be with you 'cause you make my heart scream and holler.

4
I got nine lives, cat's eyes. Abusin' every one of them and running wild.

5 The soft chant of new-born singing,

The magic force of your feelings.

6
I started to enjoy the poetry and symphonies. I took it in my stride.

7 I've had a million different offers on the phone...

But I just stayed right here at home.

8 All the school kids so sick of books,

They like the punk and the metal band.

9
Words mean so little,
and money less,
When you're lying next to me.

10
This will be my testimony.
Show me round your fruit cage

'cause I will be your honey bee.

11
Dust my lemon lies with powder
pink and sweet The day I stop...

is the day you change and fly away from me.

13
The heat of passion is
such a beautiful thing.
As it overflows, pleasure grows.

12
Burning bright, A fire blows
the signal to the sky.
I sit and wonder, does the
message get to you?

15
I was sittin' all alone,

Watching people get it on with each other.

14
She was so in love with me, we were gonna
get wed.

So, I bought her lots of things; diamond ring,
brand new bed.

16
Enraged, incensed, there's
no reason, no sense.
Awake, a dream, in
the distance, a scream.

17
When we're together
we never fight,
We've got better
things to do tonight.

19
Under his nose was a dream come true,

Been there all the time and he almost knew.

18
Out from the skies, a thousand more will die
each day.

Death is just a heartbeat away.

20
Well, maybe this could be the
ending with nothing left of you.
A hundred wishes couldn't
say, I don't want to.

Growing Up With Jamie Days:

When he was eleven years old, **Jamie Days** began to keep a day-to-day account of his life growing up in a Yorkshire village. Here he shares some of his diary entries from the mid-Eighties.

Wednesday 11th January 1984
Today was alright but nothing really happened. I asked Sarah out just because everybody else was asking people out. First she said "I'll think about it", next she said "yes". Payney is going out with Tracy.

Thursday 12th January
We got some stupid homework to look in a newspaper for news articles. I've chucked Sarah. We had an ace time with that stupid teacher [Mrs Hollings]. We said that we were going on strike. We had an IQ test. I don't think it was fair. Payney chucked Tracy.

Monday 16th January
Jason was really rude to Mrs Hollings. In Science he was mucking about and then he was asked a question. He didn't know what we were talking about. He was told to come and sit at the front. He said "no". She said come and sit here or go sit outside Mr Brown's classroom. He said, "I don't want to". In the end, he said that he'd decided to go and sit at the front. Carl ate a sweet in lesson time.

Tuesday 17th January
I bought 10 lasers and got 15p selling 5 of them. Jason refused to let Mrs Hollings look after his jumper. At cubs we went on an assault course. It was fandabbydosy.

Wednesday 25th January

Mr Brooke accused me of sending love letters to Claire but really it was to Claire and Co's Claire'll Fix It scheme. He is not exactly in my good books. Jason lost his Maths book. Mr Brooke bollocked him … he has to stand outside Mr Brooke's office and do some work. I think that is unfair. I have got terrible stomach pains. It has forecast snow.

Friday 27th January

Everybody wanted to know why I wasn't at school yesterday. Bought Mum a plant and a cup for her birthday. The plant should have cost 75p but Mrs Pullan said I could have it for 70p with a gift card. Good going, eh?

Tuesday 21st February

Cubs today. I suppose it was alright. I had a funny day at school today. I did fancy hairstyles. All my fringe was flicked up. Mrs Marshall told me to comb it down in break. It wasn't fair.

Friday 8th June

I got loads of homework. The Milk Race came past school. I got two 'I've got a lotta bottle' stickers and a hat. Me and Peter rode on Duncan's milk float. Only round the cul-de-sacs though. I gave Duncan a sticker for his milk float. Mum put the other one on the fridge next to her 'I Love Bruno' one.

Tuesday 12th June

Everything rubbish at school. Today Mrs Hollings said we are going on a school trip to … she wouldn't tell us! She said we have to wait until tomorrow. I got RE homework.

Wednesday 13th June

Went to a pub at school. That was the surprise. It was crap. We also got marched 3 miles in the pouring rain just to pick bloody flowers.

Friday 22nd June

Nit Nurse came today. She asked me if I had problems with my ears. I said "pardon?". Had our French exam. It was frightening. Did my pendant in CDT.

Friday 28th September

Mr Smith did assembly today about 'Pride in the Name of Love' and played it twice. It is about Judas and Jesus. I got done in Science by Mr Dunn. I got a C for my experiment write up and got spellings as well for Bunsen Burner.

Saturday 29th September

Mum went berserk with me about my Science homework. She has written a message to Mr Dunn in my book and I had to do it again and was not allowed to play out. It is so unfair and she is so embarrassing.

Growing Up With Jamie Days

Friday 2nd November
All the boys got kept back after assembly and Mr. Brooke read a passage from the bible about he who pisseth on the wall. We all cracked up. Some boys have been peeing up the wall to see who can get it the highest. Not me!

Thursday 29th November
I hit Carl with my Bubbalicious ruler and it snapped. I am mad with him. We all watched the Band Aid video. Mum went on about Bananarama for looking miserable. She thinks the record and Bob Geldof are brilliant.

Thursday 13th December
I went round to Marky's after school and stayed until his bedtime. We watched Top of the Pops to see 'Nellie the Elephant'. 'Like A Virgin' was on too I love it. Mr R didn't like it though. He's a stiff and so embarrassing when he tries to do the 'Nellie the Elephant' dance.

Monday 7th January 1985
Back to school. It was boring. We had to do cross country run in Games, and it was snowing and freezing!

I came third to last but only cos I walked when Thorpey wasn't looking. Tristan coughed up blood!

Wednesday 30th January
Got my photos back from school, they are mega! The ones I thought would be really good are OK but there's an ace one of the class dossing about where Bernie is punching Carl in the face. Exams were OK. Me and Justin got semi-done when we were queuing up cos we were singing "I wanna know what love is, I want you to show me, I wanna feel what love is, I want you to feel me" really loudly and Mr Brooke heard us. When he'd gone we all just cracked up!

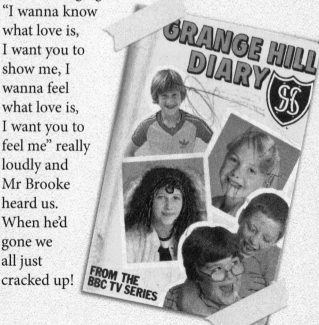

ORANGE HILL DIARY

FROM THE BBC TV SERIES

Thursday 7th March
Had a good idea to do something about the Miners' strike for my Coal Industry topic. Well, it was Dad's idea, but I agreed. He highlighted all the important dates from this thing in the Yorkshire Post and I copied them out. Did 7 pages! It took ages but I did it watching TV.

Friday 26th April
We are definitely going on strike. Everybody wants to do it. We just need to choose the day and get the others to do it when they are back from Arran. In Science we started lifecycles with the amoeba so it's sex education soon!

Wednesday 12th June
We all got the day off school because there was a teachers' strike. Went with Nikki and Mazz and their mum and dad to York. We went to the Jorvik museum. I used my Blue Peter badge to get in free. It was really short and not that good really. I bought 'Crazy For You'. It's mega - even mum likes it.

Tuesday 14th January
Today in Integrated Studies, Thorpey confiscated my Madonna scarf. He asked me why I liked her and I said "because she's fit, isn't she?" He didn't understand. He said "Why? Does she do lots of sport?" We just laughed. In Science we did experiments with sulphuric acid and metals. It was brilliant. Me and Justin splattered acid up the wall and it all went yellow. Not a lot else today.

Wednesday 5th February
I hate Mr Dodgeson. He made me take off my Madonna bracelets because he says they aren't part of school uniform. He's a right fascist. Emma bought her camera to school today. She got me to take photos of the boys getting changed. I got Nick Babb, Bernie and Wally. It was a right laugh. We went to have my hair cut at Fuzzy's. It's totally revolting. Mum says she likes it but I don't. God knows what everyone will say at school it's miles too short. It cost £4 too. I want it streaked.

Friday 7th February
It carried on snowing on and off today so we all played out in at school again. To rebel against Mr Dodgeson I'm wearing my Madonna bracelets under my jumper. Today Mr Guernsey accused us of stealing from the store cupboard in the CDT room. That has really got me. I mean who would want to steal a centre punch? Had science test today. I think I did well.

WOULDN'T IT BE GOOD TO CATCH UP WITH NIK KERSHAW?

An ever-present force in the UK charts in 1984, with three Top 10 singles '*Wouldn't It Be Good*', '*I Won't Let The Sun Go Down On Me*' and '*The Riddle*', and two Top 10 albums, **Nik Kershaw** launched his musical career in a way many musicians can only dream of doing. Enjoying further chart success during the mid-Eighties, with songs including '*Wide Boy*' and '*Don Quixote*', it is little wonder he has remained a firm favourite with fans of the Eighties, regularly playing gigs and festivals. I caught up with the singer, songwriter and multi-instrumentalist ahead of his performance at this year's Jack Up The 80s festival.

How does performing now compare to performing in the Eighties?
"It's a lot more fun now, to be honest. It seems like there's less at stake... it doesn't seem so terribly important. It's just something I do, and I enjoy doing it. I have fun doing it."

The retro circuit continues to thrive. Why do you think that 80's music has retained its popularity?
"I don't know exactly, but I remember buying records back then and it was a big deal, going to buy an album, taking it home, listening to it, reading the sleeve notes and all of that. I think people got more engaged with the music back then. It had more invested in it. So, they have kind of carried it with them through their lives, whereas nowadays it seems all very disposable. Music's like something that goes on in the background while you're doing something else. It has less value, I think. Maybe that's it? Maybe people are harking back to that golden age.

And maybe a generation that refuses to grow old?
"Yeah... but why would that be any different from the Seventies or Nineties? Because you'd think a decade's revival would last about a decade, wouldn't you? But the Eighties keeps going. The Seventies have faded out and the Nineties aren't really taking over."

One of my theories about the strength of Eighties music is that it is due to so many songs back then containing a message, whether or not we were aware of that message. In fact, I often cite 'I Won't Let The Sun Go Down On Me' as being an example of that theory — perfect pop that is actually about nuclear war. Have we lost that with today's music?
"Well, what you hear through the mass media is really quite generic and throwaway, but there's lots of good stuff out there. I don't think it's necessarily about the music, it's more about the way we consume it and listen to it. It's changed so much over the years because of the internet and everything."

How have you adapted to those changes in the music industry over the last thirty years?
"I don't even consider myself part of the music business anymore. I just play my guitar and sing my songs, so it hasn't really changed [for me]. I still do that. Not much has changed because my audience as come with me really. A lot of it has just happened, and it's not like you can get the toothpaste back in the tube. It's out there and this is the way it is now. You just have to get on with it."

Along with Go West and Cutting Crew, you are part of the 'Icons of The 80s' tour which begins in the UK in January 2018. Do you have anyone you would like to collaborate with?
"I don't. I think we're all off doing our own things, and certainly not from that era. I've always been a bit of a control freak and just enjoy doing my own thing. I spent most of the Nineties writing with and for other people, so I've kind of been through that."

Nik wrote Chesney Hawkes' debut single 'The One And Only', which topped the UK charts for five weeks in 1991. I ask if we will hear the song later.
"You might well, yes." [Nik laughs] "It's such a big hit I can't really not play it. It's such a good festival song."

Do you have a favourite song you like to perform?
"I've never got tired of singing 'Wouldn't It Be Good'. Over the years, you mess about with the songs 'cause you kind of get bored playing them the same way all the time. I've changed some of them so they're almost unrecognisable sometimes, playing them acoustic or a totally different arrangement. Because I've been doing a lot of the revival things, they've come back because a lot of people want to hear the record, don't they? So, they've gone back to that. But 'Wouldn't It Be Good' never went through that cycle. It was always the same... just bashing the chords out! It's a good, fun song to play."

Can you pick out one highlight of the Eighties for you?
"There were so many. People might expect me to say Live Aid but it really wasn't. It was such a stressful day. It was obviously such a massive event to put on, and I'm privileged to have been part of it, but it wasn't the greatest gig I've ever played. There were just lots of really great gigs and those odd moments when you're really just there… just present. It's probably about halfway through a tour, when you really know what you're doing, you don't have to think about it too much. It's just there and you're part of it… this one great, amazing moment. Those moments, I don't think you can beat those."

Is there anything you miss about the Eighties?
"Not really. I miss my youth! I miss walking up and down stairs without getting out of puff… that kind of thing."

Who inspired you to go into music?
"David Bowie. There used to be a programme called Nationwide in the late Seventies. It was about twenty minutes… a magazine programme… arts and features. One of them was this thing on Bowie on his Ziggy Stardust tour. I thought 'what's going on?'. I'd never seen or heard anything like that. It was amazing. There was always a guitar in our house. I never figured out why there was a guitar in our house. It was a horrible nylon strung guitar but it had steel strings on it. It was almost impossible to play, and someone had painted it with white emulsion, but it was always there and I'd never bothered to pick it up. But that's when I picked it up and started messing about with it. Then I bought an actual electric guitar which I plugged into the radiogram, because it had an amp, and that's what started me off."

Had you considered any other career before going into music?
"Before that, I wanted to be an actor. I was in drama groups and always wanted to show off on the stage somehow."

Have you ever thought about combining an acting career with music, like some of your contemporaries have done?
"A lot of pop stars like to think they'd be good at acting because of all those videos we did for MTV. They liked to put in a little thirty second performance before the song starts. One of those was on 'Wide Boy' and I was required to do some acting. I remember watching it back and thinking 'Oh my god, that's just awful'. It's not quite as easy as it looks, is it? So, I thought 'You know what? I'm probably not going to be in the movies!'"

We've come to my final question, and it's probably the most important one I have to ask you. Will you ever wear a snood again in your lifetime?
"I can pretty much guarantee, no!" [Nik laughs]. "That all happened by accident somehow… this bizarre connection I've got with that garment. It was only for a few mad weeks, when it was all really intense, and it was photo session, after photo session, after photo session. I hated that photograph. I looked like a cuddly toy. I just really hated it, and thought I'd got rid of every copy of that photograph. We travelled right the way across the world. I got to Australia and the big kind of Top of The Pops programme there, Countdown I think it was called. We walked onto the set and they'd actually festooned the whole studio with massive pictures of it. I had a little hissy fit and asked them to take them down, but they wouldn't. I think they did in the end. They relented!"

NIK KERSHAW   MCA RECORDS

80'S SWEETS AND TREATS WORDSEARCH

```
G R A P L Y S U D E C A P S L S H P U A
O E O J N R A B I S C U I A T J R P N I
F D U S T I A O R I A S R T U K A A B C
F C O C E N R E M B S O O U B C B R T O
O K C E J K C A P S A N M M B A Y R B J
T R E O N A N A B I U G O B C Y T A A N
Q A C S P A N N K A R G B C A Q T U N A
I U K S K A T E U I E D E T I N U Q A R
Z Q T N X X L R Z T I D K N D K N A U O
B U B E F L U F F Y T Z F T E T R A T A
R Y T Z F A Q N R N Y B L E I R R S T S
F Y S H U B B A B U B B A D P Z Z E R S
Y F E O T A A N A I I A R Y P I E J D T
F T S U D U M N X H U T A B U T G R U E
B W G S T S U D E C A P S O P S I K O E
A O B R E W M X T N B B U B H O R S E R
C W I B B A B B U H S H U L S U N I T T
N O I R B B O A L S O R T A U Q P U D E
C A L F T A N K A I O R I A L O A N E Z
I I A P O M G L P F R U I T S K A O R A
N K C E D P O T E X A S S C A B A N S N
```

Banjo	Cabana	Hubba Bubba
Kia-Ora	Nutty Bar	Opal Fruits
Pacers	Quatro	Slush Puppie
Space Dust	Texan	Tizer
Toffo	Top Deck	Treets
Trio	Um Bongo	United

CRY ME A RIVER

The first time a tune brings a tear to your eye can be the first real connection you make with music. I asked some 80's artists 'What was the first song to make you cry?'

Dave Wakeling:
"The first song that made me cry was 'Ruby Tuesday'. That's the time when music makes its first deep bite into you, when you make a connection with it. I was coming home from a swimming gala and I'd won, which meant I could sit in the back of the car with an orange pop, the radio on, and a present out of the boot, whilst my dad went in to celebrate my great victory with three or four swift halves. If I lost, I sat in the park 'til it was dark. Even a silver was failure. You've been in the pool all day, so you're all chlorinated and stingy eyes anyway. The radio was on and it played 'Walk Away Renee' by The Four Tops, which is very emotional anyway, and then 'Ruby Tuesday'. That was it... gone.

I remember it was like my whole body was tingling. All my nerves were prickling all over my body. It was the first time I'd ever felt anything as strong as the high from swimming training, when you'd think 'I can't swim anymore, it's hurting so much and I can't breathe'. Then, all of a sudden, it was like you were swimming in slow motion. It was a bit like drugs," Dave grins "from what people tell me. It's certainly like adrenalin is involved, and probably seratonin too."

Johnny Logan:
"Whoa, that's an unusual question. The first song to make me cry … there have been so many songs that have had that effect. I'm one of these people that does get very emotional. I still get very emotional when I listen to 'Adagio For Strings' by Samuel Barber.

I think when I first heard 'The Dance' by Garth Brooks that had an effect on me, because I realised it was about somebody who had passed away. 'Hold Me Now' I sang at my aunt's, who was like a second mother to me, funeral. I just did it with an acoustic guitar, and had a good weep after that. 'Danny Boy' always does it to me too. When something touches me, it really does touch me and I kind of well up a bit."

Nik Kershaw:
"Wow, that's a good one! I don't think it was a song, I think it was a piece of classical music. One of my parents' LPs was Enigma Variations by Elgar. One of the movements on there was Nimrod.

It's an amazing tune. Holst as well … The Planets suite, Jupiter … some of the music in there has brought me to tears. I must admit, I was in a sad place at the time but it's the stuff that makes your hairs stand up."

Eddi Reader:

"I got my dad to write the words of 'Love Me Tender' by Elvis Presley. My dad is a massive Elvis Presley fan, so when he came home from work one day, covered in welding grease in his fingernails, he was writing out the words for me. There's about seven verses to that bloody song, but he wrote it out: "Love me tender, love me long, take me to your heart," sings Eddi. He said "What do you want that for?" and I said "I'm going to sing it in school." So, I graduated from singing in the closes with all the other girls and boys to taking it to the next level.

I put my hand up and said to Miss MacDonald "Yes, I'd like to sing this time." So, she got me up. She couldn't quite believe it, that I would be singing. There was a bit of tittering and what not, and then I started singing 'Love Me Tender'. I shut my eyes and the tears were streaming out of them. I couldn't hold it in, I was so nervous. I had my hands behind my head and I leaned against the blackboard, hoping for it to hold me up, just against the wall there. I shut my eyes and I sung the whole thing," Eddi tells me proudly. "At the end of it, I opened them and they were all open-mouthed. They all wanted to walk me home, and the teacher was like "I didn't know you had such a beautiful voice, Sadenia." That was the first song that made me cry, and I knew that it would make me cry. I knew I couldn't hold it in."

Nick van Eede:

"My brother died about six years ago, and when we were teenagers my dad was a mobile DJ. He was kind of naff but good. Gary and I would hump his gear for him. So, about 11 o'clock in the evening, we'd come off our pub night and go and help Dad with the gear. Always towards the end of his disco nights, he would play 'Misty Blue' by Dorothy Moore. That made me cry back then. It was just a beautiful song."

David Ball:

"That's a good question. The first song that made me cry … it's got to be something to do with me breaking up with a girlfriend. I think it's probably that Diana Ross one that goes "da na na na na" [I'm Still Waiting]. Yeah, it's probably that.

It was when I split up with a girlfriend. That was one of our favourite songs, when I was a teenager, so that was a bit of a weepy moment."

Peter Coyle:

"Probably 'A Boy Named Sue' by Johnny Cash or Charlie Rich 'The Most Beautiful Girl'. My dad, he had a hard life, but on a Sunday morning he'd put on these country tunes."

Martyn Ware:

"'A Man Needs A Maid' by Neil Young... the lyrics, the poignant way he expresses his vulnerability in a 'stoic' way really resonated with me as a young man trying to understand my own identity."

Jay Aston:

"I think it was 'The Great Gig In The Sky' by Pink Floyd. It's just got that amazing vocal. My brother used to come 'round two or three nights a week, and we'd listen to Wishbone Ash, Focus and Pink Floyd... all that heavy, intense, semi-prog music, and that one really stood out."

Mike Nolan:

"Sad music! 'Climb Every Mountain'."

Bobby McVay:

"The first time I heard Frank Sinatra sing 'My Way', it made me cry. The lyrics just hit me at that time. I was probably about 13. My aunt had just moved to Australia, and they were a big family, a bit like the Partridge Family, always playing guitars and singing. They taught me how to play the guitar, so around that time I got quite emotional."

16

Cheryl Baker:

"I can't remember the first song that made me cry but I do remember going to see Les Mis for the first time, and weeping like a baby all the way through. Now, anytime I hear any song that says 'I love you' or 'I'm dying' I start crying."

Jona Lewie:

"That's a good question... really good question that is. I can remember more recently, a record by Neil Diamond, 'I Am I Said'. It's just very emotional and I think that latterly, in the last twenty odd years, there are more and more lyrics now that are sensational for crying to. A lot of country music's like that. That's one that I remember, and there are others, but I never cried to all my early influences, I have to say. It was just the feeling of it, and not so much the lyrical thing. It was the music, the melody and the vibe in the backing track."

Junior Giscombe:

"It was 'A Change Is Gonna Come' by Sam Cooke."

Sally-Ann Triplett:

"This is really embarrassing. That would be 'Where Is Love?' from 'Oliver'," laughs Sally-Ann. "My friend and I used to dress up. She used to come 'round to my house and we had two dresses, a red one and a green one. I always gave her the green one because you couldn't kick your legs in it, but the red one was great. You could kick your legs right high. We used to sit and listen to 'Oliver' and 'Where Is Love?' and cry. I think we must have forced ourselves to cry. I don't think it was an actual cry. It was a theatrical, lying in my red dress cry!"

TEN GOOD QUESTIONS FOR JASON DONOVAN

First coming to our attention in 1986, when he took over the role of Scott Robinson in the Australian soap Neighbours, **Jason Donovan** went on to launch his career in music two years later with his Stock Aitken & Waterman produced debut single '*Nothing Can Divide Us*', which reached number five in the UK charts. Swiftly followed by a string of hits, including three chart toppers: '*Especially For You*', a duet with Kylie Minogue, '*Too Many Broken Hearts*' and '*Sealed With A Kiss*', a cover of the 1962 Brian Hyland track, the tail end of the Eighties proved to be a golden era for the Melbourne-born boy who would go on to wear an amazing technicolour dreamcoat in the lead role of Joseph, in Andrew Lloyd Webber's West End stage production in 1991.

Currently combining singing, acting and presenting the 80s Rewind show for Heart Radio, Jason took a break from his hectic schedule to answer a few questions.

You appear to have embraced the retro circuit. How does performing now compare to when you first started out in music?
I think that performing now, for me, comes with a lot more ease. That's the great thing about getting a bit older, you feel more comfortable in your own skin and worry less. The 80's circuit is great because it's always full of familiar faces and we get to sing the songs we've all grown up with.

How have changes within the music industry over the last thirty years affected you as an artist?
I don't think they've affected me directly, as the majority of my music career happened before iTunes, streaming and social media were around. In some ways the world is smaller because you can have access to everything at all times, but in other ways it's bigger because there are so many different routes to go down and get yourself out there. I certainly think it's a lot harder for young artists now to push through than when I was starting out in music.

How important to you is it to have a balance between your acting and singing careers? Do you favour one over the other, or does your ideal working life blend the two?
I really enjoy both for different reasons. Acting is where I started and opened doors that gave me the opportunities to make music, which undoubtedly changed my life. When I was working with Stock Aiken & Waterman, it was a really exciting time which defined a whole generation of music, and I feel very thankful that I'm still able to sing those songs that bring back so many memories for all of us. That's something really special. That said, I love the challenges that acting brings and the places that taking on a new character takes me to. I can't pick one or the other as I get so much from both!

" I feel very thankful that I'm still able to sing those songs that bring back so many memories for all of us.

Knowing what you do now, what advice would you give to the 20-year-old Jason Donovan about to embark on his career in music?
Pace yourself, take a few more risks, eat well, avoid self-indulgence and temptation of drugs and alcohol and try and keep a balance. I don't know whether I would have changed my life much, but I certainly would have been a bit more patient with things and I would have spent more time writing and developing ideas.

In addition to singing and acting, you also present the 80s Rewind show on Heart Radio on Sunday evenings. Is it fun dipping back into the Eighties every week?
I love presenting my Heart show. I've been doing it quite a while now, and not only has it taught me another form of working with music, but who wouldn't want to listen to those songs every week? It's a real pleasure and never fails to bring back a lot of memories.

Is there anything you miss about the Eighties?
When we talk about the Eighties, people get really nostalgic and I'm no different. It was a great time, full of excitement and possibility, where new things were emerging all the time. Music is certainly one of the biggest things that we immediately associate with the Eighties, and I'm so happy to have been part of it. I don't know that I miss anything — perhaps maybe the mullet!

What are your five favourite songs from the Eighties?
'Waiting For A Star To Fall' by Boy Meets Girl, 'Boys Don't Cry' by The Cure, anything by New Order, anything by Heaven 17 and anything from 'The Joshua Tree' album by U2.

Hmmm, that's slightly more than five songs! What was the first single you ever bought?
'Coming Up' by Paul McCartney.

Can you remember what was the first song to make you cry?
I'm a bit of a wimp when it comes to music, [probably] Peter Gabriel 'Don't Give Up' or 'Red Rain' or Tears For Fears' 'Woman in Chains'.

You once sang 'Any Dream Will Do', so can you describe your dream day?
It has to be making the house look nice, setting the table and having a nice lunch with friends, a glass of champagne, watching a bit of TV, maybe some football in the afternoon. We have a house out of town and I love to sit on my lawnmower and potter around in the garden. It's the simple things that make life perfect.

10 GOOD THINGS ABOUT 1988

Thirty years on, author of 'The Top 40 Annual 1988' **James Masterton** tells us why 1988 was such a great year.

1 Kylie was invented.

Before 1988 started Kylie Minogue was Charlene Mitchell, the tomboy mechanic from 'Neighbours' who was busy getting romantic with Jason Donovan's Scott Robinson in episodes they had seen in Australia a year and half earlier. We had kind of heard rumours that she had been a big deal in the Australian pop charts too, but never imagined she would amount to anything over here. Then came 'I Should Be So Lucky', storming into the winter charts like a golden ray of sunshine. It stayed at the top for five weeks, turning her into a household name and launching a singing and performing career that would see her remain a superstar for over 25 years. By the end of 1988, her debut album 'Kylie' had sold over two million copies in Britain alone. Extraordinarily, that was only the beginning.

2 House Music became a thing.

Previous years had seen the occasional club record creep into the charts, strange sounding creations from America all using a catchy piano rhythm, but nobody really had a name for them. Then in 1988 it was like a cork had popped. It seemed as if every other new entry on the Top 40 was a track you could dance to. Melody and lyrics were optional, but including the word "House" in the title was clearly helpful: 'Rok Da House', 'The Jack That House Built', 'House Arrest'. All were smashes. Then there was Bomb The Bass who made 'Beat Dis', that strange collection of sounds and voices, all of which seemed to be propelled by the same beeping made by your digital alarm clock. It might even have topped the charts, but for Kylie (see above). By the end of the year we had moved on to Acid House, as Jolly Roger and Humanoid made their machines chirp and bleep at high speed. Life as a pop fan would truly never be the same again.

3 Novelty hits were EVERYWHERE

Every year of the Eighties had its occasional fun, quirky records. 1988 had LOADS. Harry Enfield had a hit as Loadsamoney, Newcastle comedians Star Turn On 45 (Pints) parodied House Music with 'Pump Up The Bitter', Morris Minor and The Majors were all doing the 'Stutter Rap' and we ended the year with A Tribe Of Toffs telling us how 'John Kettley Is A Weatherman' - and so was Wincey Willis, they added. One of them even made Number One: The Timelords (later to become better known as The KLF) mashed up Gary Glitter with the Dr Who theme song and almost by accident landed one of the more extraordinary chart-topping singles of the year. They even wrote a book claiming to unlock the secret of how to repeat the trick.

4 Let's hear it for the girls

How did you land a hit single in 1988? Well, being female and barely 21 was a good way to start. As well as Kylie (who was only 19 at the start of the year), we saw the first hits for Debbie Gibson (just 17), Sabrina chirped about boys, in a bikini which didn't fit her (20) and pouting redhead Tiffany made it all the way to the top of the charts with 'I Think We're Alone Now', just a few months after her 16th birthday. Yet every single one of them was trumped by a 15 year old schoolgirl from France, and we didn't even have a clue what she was singing.

5 Your French teacher got into pop music

Vanessa Paradis was her name, and her exotic tale of a taxi driver turned jazz star Joe Le Taxi raced up the charts in February, just as she had in her home country the previous summer. It meant pop music moved from the common room to the classroom as French teachers across the land leaped on the chance to (finally!) get even the laziest child interested in languages as they devoted lessons to translating the lyrics. Then, just as the song had died away, along came another – 'Voyage Voyage' by Desireless and her tale of sacred Indian Oceans and flying carpets. We translated that too, but it still didn't make any sense.

6 It invented Paloma Faith (sort of)

Australian rock band INXS were busy releasing singles from their 'Kick' album but, frustratingly, nobody in Britain really got them in the same way the Americans did. Almost unnoticed was the summertime ballad 'Never Tear Us Apart', which crept to Number 24 in July. Somebody who later went into advertising was a fan though, and the song resurrected 24 years later in a new version sung by Paloma Faith. The soundtrack to a John Lewis advert, it reached the Top 20 at a time when even she was struggling to be noticed. At which point we all claimed to have loved the original back in the day.

7 Bros were the biggest

Their first releases in 1987 had flopped, yet as 1988 dawned there was suddenly a new pop group sensation on the block. Perhaps loved just as much for their looks as their music, Bros were literally every teenage girl's dream. Twins Matt and Luke Goss had chiselled jaws, waxed and spiky blonde hair and spoke endlessly about how they loved the "fans". There was even their mate Craig who perhaps wasn't quite as pretty but got fancied too out of pity. There were hits: 'When Will I Be Famous', 'Drop The Boy' and Number One smash 'I Owe You Nothing', but it was also all about the screaming, the jeans, the shoes accessorised with Grolsch bottle tops (beg your Dad to drink one and give it to you), and even more screaming. They ended the year back near the top of the charts singing 'Silent Night', just as you did at school. Okay, it didn't last and everyone quickly moved on but, for a time, being a Brosette was more or less compulsory.

8 The Pet Shop Boys were imperial

Chris Lowe himself once said it. They had had the 1987 Christmas Number One with 'Always On My Mind' and, for the next 12 months, the Pet Shop Boys could do practically no wrong. They shot to the top of the charts again at Easter with 'Heart' and even managed to find the time to turn Patsy Kensit into the proper pop star she had always dreamed of being, writing and producing 'I'm Not Scared' for Eighth Wonder. Then came the summer and the sultry 'Domino Dancing', their album 'Introspective' which may only have had six tracks but still became their biggest ever seller - rounding things off with the majestic Left To My Own Devices. The hits would continue to roll on for decades and the duo would remain rightly famous well into the 21st century, but 1988 was the year when everything they touched turned to gold. It was an amazing time to be a fan.

9 Billy Bragg topped the charts (but nobody noticed)

The New Musical Express sponsored the recording of a charity album 'Sgt Pepper Knew My Father', which saw a huge range of contemporary acts all take turns at recording new versions of the songs from the Beatles' famous 'Sgt Pepper's Lonely Hearts Club Band' record. Most attention was paid to the hit single, 'With A Little Help From My Friends', recorded by Wet Wet Wet and which topped the charts for four weeks, raising even more money for Childline. But this was a double-sided hit, and Billy Bragg's recording of 'She's Leaving Home' had equal billing. So, technically the Bard of Barking had a Number One hit too - he even performed it on Top Of The Pops. Yet you will struggle to find many people who can actually remember it, and he never came close to doing so again.

10 A Coca-Cola advert topped the charts

"You said let's share a Coke, something new had begun" sang the shrill-voiced American lady on the TV adverts, which seemed to be everywhere during the summer. Impossibly good-looking teenagers walked impossibly hot-looking streets and stole kisses over bottles of sticky teeth-rotting pop, all soundtracked by an intense rock ballad. Yet, when the song was released towards the end of the year, we just couldn't get enough of it. Robin Beck was the lady's name and her one and only international hit record was the full version of the Coke jingle 'First Time'. Cutting a swathe through the House records and Kylie hits, it reached the very top of the charts, just as the New Seekers had done with their own Coca-Cola advert record a decade and a half earlier. Now where did I put my air guitar?

For more information on James and his books visit www.masterton.co.uk/books

TOP 40 ANNUAL 1988
James Masterton

Growing Up With Jamie Days

Sunday 5th February 1984

Nothing happened today although I went swimming in the morning to Otley swimming baths. It was alright but the changing rooms were horrible. You didn't even have a cubicle to yourself you had to walk around nude. Two girls came in there was well! Mum and Dad went out to Texas to get some things for the bathroom. Nikki came round. It was boring.

Saturday 10th March

I went to John's party today. We went to the Green Frog. I didn't like it at all. John was dead peevish with his money. His cake had rum in. There was a picture of a nude woman in the bogs. Today was so terribly boring.

Thursday 5th July

In French found out about French trip. Mum and Dad say I can go. It costs £70. In the coach there are videos!

Wednesday 25th July

Me & Katie wrote to Jim'll Fix It. She asked to meet Bucks Fizz and I asked for a day out in London with a chimpanzee. I will get picked, I know it.

Wednesday 8th August

Me and John took a barrel down to the school field to roll it down the hill with us inside it. He went first but it bounced like mad and wouldn't stop. His head was hanging out the end and he was shouting "stop it" and screaming "help!". I was laughing but was dead scared and couldn't stop him. He cried and shouted at me and went home and I had to take the barrel back by myself, then I had no one to play with.

Thursday 9th August

Inflatables today but it was in the church hall because of the weather. It was not as good as last year. They didn't play 'Fame' once and there was no one to help me back on the donut one this time either. John is in a nark with me because of yesterday. He says it was my idea. It was but he could've said 'no', the wazzock.

Saturday 8th September
Day quite boring. Played with Marky at his house.
I did my Roland Rat impression and really made
him laugh. He laughed so much until he peed
on the settee. He got into trouble and I got sent
home. Hee Heee Rat Fans!!!!

Thursday 13th September
We didn't do Integrated Studies, we did about
what we are doing in France. We set off at 11.00
tonight. I am waiting to go now.

Friday 14th September
The coach journey to France was hell. No one
could get to sleep because people at the back like
Kingy and Jeremy Thompson kept talking. Me
and Emma and Sally had just got to sleep on the
floor when Sayers shouted "we're here" but it was
just the ferry port. At a garage Justin banged a can
of coke on the ground. It went everywhere! I fell
asleep on the ferry and Alistair reckoned he put
his finger in my mouth when they walked past
- bet he didn't. We had a room with two double
beds and a bunk bed. I shared with Bernie. On
the first night I thought I saw a skeleton sat up in
one of the beds. I was shit scared.

Saturday 15th September
Went to see the Bayeux Tapestry. It was crap; it
was really short. I bought a postcard strip of it
but it wasn't even of the whole thing and I got
some cola spice on a string. In the afternoon we
had to look round a village for the prices of stuff
but everything was shut. It was boring. I bought
a Smurf baby. I thought it was 1f 25c but it was
12f 50c! I have hardly any money left. When we
got back to the hotel our room smelt of shit. It
is above the kitchen and that was our tea! It was
meat and everyone said it was horse so no one
would eat it! I ate everyone's stuffed tomatoes.

Growing Up With Jamie Days

Sunday 16th September

In the morning we went to see a load of war graves. There were hundreds of white crosses all in massive rows. I got mad with Thompson because he was running about on them and being a knob head and it made the girls cry. It is a cemetery for God's sake! On the way back we stopped at a beach and went in the sea. My balls were freezing! All day the teachers were on about us having a disco for the last night but all it was was a tape recorder and one tape! Mrs Richardson tried to make me dance. I refused.

We all just dossed about outside the hotel. We had a right laugh. But at night we were all messing about in the room jumping off the bunk bed and onto the other beds and the elastic snapped in Justin's pyjama bottoms! We were all laughing cos they just kept falling down and Mrs Hartley came in. She bollocked us for how we behaved and said they would send letters home and that we are never allowed on any school trips ever again. That is all of us except Grovey! Bernie cried but Alistair thought it was funny! I was bricking it!

Monday 17th September

Everyone got bollocked this morning because some people had bought French bangers, and they are illegal in England. They were told to hand them in. It was Beefy and Payney I reckon. Also some bubble gum got on Mrs Richardson's skirt, so that is banned too. I had bought some of the kind that is in tubes but handed it in because of last night.

We went to a Hypermarket. I bought some camembert for Mum and some grenadine that Alistair said makes milkshakes. I burnt my tongue on hot chocolate on the ferry. We went in the gambling bit but you're not supposed to. It was ace but I am glad to be home.

Sunday 24th March 1985

I had David N, Katie, Vicky, Nikki and Mazz in. We all had coke floats. They were mega! Everyone had a go on the Sodastream. I was allowed to stay up and watch That's Life because it was all about Ben Hardwick. It was sad. Was allowed to watch Spitting Image as well because I said I can't get to sleep because Sean and dad laugh and keep me awake. It was OK.

Saturday 4th May

Emma and David came tonight to watch The Poseidon Adventure and the Eurovision Song Contest. It was dead funny. We were doing foreign accents and saying "nil pwah" to everyone. They stayed until 10.30. Norway won, we came 4th.

Saturday 6th July

Went to Nick Babb's disco tonight. It was in his garage. There was no one else I knew there and a lot of the people were 4th years. It was okay cos they were playing good records except Sister Sledge and 'Ben' but then they wanted to play a game called kiss cuddle or grope. I asked what grope meant and this girl shouted "oh my god, he says "what's grope?". I hate her. I still don't know because I said I didn't want to play. Was glad when Dad came and picked me up.

Get busy with the fizzy SodaStream

Cutting to the chase with Nick Van Eede

The day after Cutting Crew's lead singer and songwriter Nick van Eede received an award from the BMI (Broadcast Music, Inc.) for selling over 4 million copies of '(I Just) Died In Your Arms Tonight', he met with me to discuss the song and the success it had brought him. Before we spoke about his memories of the Eighties, we travelled a little further back to discover what had inspired his initial interest in music.

When did you first pick up a guitar?
"I was 10 or 11 years old, and saw a flamenco player in Spain with my dad, on holiday in Benidorm. And bless my dad, he never had a penny… he was a builder… but he'd got this horrible, black guitar waiting for me when I got home. I couldn't even play it, it was so horrible… it was a plank! But that was what got me started. I was very lucky because I passed my eleven plus and went to the local grammar school. I hated it but one year later it went comprehensive. Suddenly, I was in this school full of student teachers and it was this whole new world, full of energetic teachers." Encouraged by his drama teacher, Nick grew in confidence and went on to perform his own songs in front of an audience for the first time.

Who were your musical influences?
"Well, I've ended up being known as the lead singer and writer for Cutting Crew so that kind of puts a stamp on things, that sound, whatever that was. I'm proud of it, you know but up until Cutting Crew I was always much harder, more New Wave, I suppose really… like The Jam meets Squeeze. Something like that, banging out these little three minute songs. I was in a band called The Drivers before Cutting Crew, and we got signed to a Canadian label. I met Kevin [MacMichael] in Canada. Really, before then it would have been Weller, and before him Marc Bolan. My first ever gig was seeing them [T-Rex] at The Dome in Brighton. I think it was me and about two thousand girls! I just loved his music. I was talking to a mate the other day about 'Electric Warrior', which I think was their best album. It just sounded great."

What type of music were you playing when started your music career as a solo artist?
"Pretty awful stuff, probably," he jokes. "I'd been the guy who sits in the corner of pubs [playing guitar] for about two years, cutting my teeth, and I was good at it. Not everybody's good at that because it's hard. You've got people playing darts or snooker, as well as your little group of fans who come along. So, you've got to keep people happy with covers, but every night I'd be slipping in another song that I'd written myself. You were learning all the time about songwriting. You're also learning about holding your own in a busy room. That always stays with me to this day. If you see me on stage, I do what I do, but if there's anything that goes a bit odd, I'm kinda prepared because all that shit happened. I remember once in a pub in Deptford, way before mobile 'phones, in maybe 79, 80. It was a really rough place. I remember turning up in my Capri, and the landlord saying "you're not going to leave it there" after I'd unloaded." Nick was told that the safest place to park his car was several streets away, which he duly did before returning to the pub to play.

"Halfway through the first set, this guy came up to me. He had this huge head and huge muscles, tattoos and everything. He said [Nick adopts a low, deep voice] "You know 'Rhinestone Cowboy' Glen Campbell." I said "Um…". He said "No, you know it" not "do you know it?". I went "Yes, I know that one, yes. I'll have a break in a minute and I'll play it in the second half." No word of a lie, I ran back to my car, drove to the nearest telephone box and called my dad, who had a good record collection. I said "For Christ sake, get me the words to 'Rhinestone Cowboy'. I'll hold on!" Nick's father gave him the lyrics, and he was able to start his second set with the request.

of cocaine or a holiday in Florida to the radio stations to get you on the radio" - were on strike. "Little Virgin, who weren't part of that, just went zoom, and seized upon the opportunity."

How much influence did video have over the band's success?
"The videos were very oblique; they didn't tell too much of a story. There wasn't too much of us in them, so when you hear '(I Just) Died In Your Arms Tonight', you don't just associate it with a video about some guy riding a horse. You just think 'Yeah, pretty cool video', but it doesn't paint too much of a picture, so you can still hear the song without [thinking of] a strong, vivid video. You want to paint your own pictures."

You went through two producers before settling on the final cut of '(I Just) Died In Your Arms Tonight'. Would you say you are a perfectionist?
"Nearly, yeah. I was very controlling then. I let things go much more now, but that's because I've got a good team around me. Back then, we weren't prepared so it was a bit panicky. I knew that this was my chance, and something could happen. I'd been doing it since I was 17… I was 26… and I knew about failure. I knew about disappointment. I knew about thinking that was going to be the big one and it wasn't. So, I was a very grown up 26-year-old, and Kevin and I were writing songs that just seemed to fit, this time for the first time ever. We were writing songs that were right for then, I looked alright for then, my voice suddenly got that 'thing'. I don't know where that came from. You listen to anything I sang up until that day, it didn't have that. I kind of knew something was lining up so… excuse my language… I was fucked if I was going to let this go. Even if they called me the biggest arsehole in the world, I was going to make this the way I thought it should happen. I wasn't a horrible person at all, but if the producer wasn't very good, it was 'get rid of this guy'!"

Do you enjoy being part of the music industry more now because you haven't got that pressure of chart success weighing on your shoulders?
"I loved it all. Everything they chucked at me, I tried to take on. Of course, it's less pressure now. You go and make a record in your own time, but there's something fantastic about being a young man in this business, and I remember it fondly. But we all had been doing it for ten years, so even though we looked like a young, fresh-faced Eighties band, we'd been around. Never trust the 'experts'. It's something I've found out since I was 15. They'll often come up to you and say 'I know what's going on here, okay? Trust me'. Usually, they're liars or they are

Your big break into music came when you supported Slade on tour in the late Seventies. How did that come about?
"Chas [Chandler] was down in the pub. He was the manager of Slade then, and the most famous man in music in the East Grinstead area, and he walked into my pub! I was playing in a hospital pub. I was the hospital orderly in the operating theatre, so I had all the nurses and doctors there partying and he walked in. That was it. He came up with his card and said 'I like what you're doing. Give me a call in the morning.' That was on a Thursday night and, I think, not the next Thursday but the following one I was in Poland, supporting Slade. That's how quick it happened."
It was also Chas Chandler who was responsible for adapting the singer/songwriter's surname. Born Nick Eede, he explains how his Dutch heritage was seen as the perfect marketing tool.

"My great grandfather was van Eede. He was Dutch," explains Nick. "I found this out when I was a boy, but just parked it up there [points to his head]. "Growing up in rural Sussex, it's not something you talk about really. When Chas signed me, he asked me to tell him about myself. He wanted to 'jazz up' my story a bit. When I told him about my grandfather, he said [adopts a Geordie accent] 'Well, that's it… Nick van fucking Eede!'. So, within two weeks it had all got 'round the village I grew up in, and my brother, his name on the football team was suddenly Gary van Eede!"

How big a part did Richard Branson play in Cutting Crew's success?
"Huge. We were signed to Siren, who were a little label under the Virgin umbrella. They gave us the hit [(I Just) Died In Your Arms Tonight] in Britain and Europe, and then America. By that time, Branson was just launching Virgin USA, and he thought that there couldn't be a better song for America to launch his label. So, we were plucked from touring in Norway and Italy and so on, to suddenly being on Hollywood Boulevard, living in the Hollywood Roosevelt Hotel. We had a number one record there, and he threw the works at us because he needed to kickstart his label.

I could see what was going on. I was under no illusion… it wasn't just 'cause he loved us. We had a tried and tested record and he wanted to make that his flagship starting point. He chose Johnny Hates Jazz as well, and T'Pau. I think we were the three Virgin bands that had had hits already, who he brought over, but we were his first number one. Even more than that, he's got that Midas touch, you know." Nick explains how Cutting Crew's rise to the top in the U.S.A. coincided with a time when the pluggers, who controlled American radio – "they would give a gram

28

not good at what they do, and got there through some other way. It's the fact that they have the arrogance to make you trust them. In the music industry, there are so many of them, and you have to weed them out or it all goes wrong and you've blown your career."

You still record and perform fresh material as well as performing on the retro circuit. How important is it to you to have that creative outlet for your new songs?
"I still make albums and that's the most important thing to me always. I think I sing better now than I did thirty years ago, so I'm very lucky to be able to still perform. Even so, the thing that I love doing is writing, recording and getting it out. It's a funny old business now and things have changed a lot, but if you offered for me to go to L.A. and play a gig in front of five thousand people or give me fifty grand to go and make an album, I'd take the album any day. I love that side. I'm a writer… always have been."

Do you have a tried and tested method for writing your songs?
"I have learned a way of getting my original ideas out. I used to find that when I drove, after about twenty miles your brain goes into some other plane. I used to get lots of ideas, not just for songs but a whole concept, because my brain would go into 'thought' mode. I thought I should tap into this for writing. I'm a good swimmer and I would swim for miles, so I now get all my ideas when I'm swimming. The latest album [Add To Favourites] is a bit of a tip of the hat to that. That's me [on the album cover] wearing a suit of armour in Lanzarote, getting out of a swimming pool. I stayed at this cheap hotel with an enormous pool. I'd swim, then a tune would come. I'd jump out, grab a towel and go back to my sunbed. There's people looking at me going [Nick sings], then I'd jump back in again. So, silly but it worked. What I need to do is get an underwater Dictaphone, so I don't have to keep on getting out!"

To continue to get such enjoyment from your writing is an achievement in itself, isn't it?
"It's been a beautiful life. The bit that really hurt, I suppose, was after the third album 'Compus Mentus' [Nick is keen to point out that the title was deliberately spelt incorrectly]. The first album sold three million, the second album sold about a million. The third album came out and, just as we were about to release it, EMI bought Virgin. Back then, it was one of the first major takeovers." Nick goes on to explain that the implication of such a move meant that the record company were "going to stiff your record, really. They released the single because that's what the contract said, but they just killed the album dead, along with 120 bands they fired that month. We were just old dross… good, but old dross. I remember saying to EMI 'Here's your money back that you've just paid me. Have it all back and give me my songs'." Despite having no intention of using Nick's songs then or in the future, his offer was rebuffed. "The reason they don't do it," he continues "is they can't bear the thought that if they gave them back to me and I got one in on the new Tom Hanks movie or something. They can't risk it. Crazy, eh?"

Do you feel the music industry is better today because artists are able to release and have control over their own material?
"Steve Earle [American singer/songwriter] was once asked in an interview, what's the difference between the music business now and when you started. He said 'The good thing about the music business now is that anybody can make an album. The bad thing about the music business now is that anybody can make an album.' When we were younger, you could discover new music. Now, there's eight million bands, how do we find it?"

Recognising that both advantages and disadvantages have arisen in the music industry over the last three decades, we move on to discuss how those changes have impacted upon songwriters financially.

"Let's put my cards on the table," says Nick. "I'm very lucky. I've got one massive hit that never stops getting played and I've got two or three others that are played all the time, all around the world. And I've got about another hundred songs published. I came from an era when the contracts were not bad, and the royalties come through, so lucky me. If I have any responsibility at all, it's to try and agitate the best I can, through PRS (Performing Right Society), BMI and MCPS (Mechanical Copyright Protection Society) to do their best, and I do. That's because I get a separate statement that comes through each month for my downloads. It's so funny because on the front page it shows you how many downloads. I see something like 12,000 [Nick claps his hands excitedly] and turn over to the last page… [where it says] eighty two pounds! You know, and that's me, with my ability to get my big songs all over the world. What if you're a new band? You're lucky to get twenty quid. That doesn't even pay for a set of strings. It's so wrong."

What other artists have you written for besides Cutting Crew?
"Mika… his 'Life In Cartoon Motion' album [which included the number one single 'Grace Kelly']. I wrote a song called 'Relax, Take It Easy' with him, which was a big hit across Europe." The track reached number 18 in the UK and topped the charts in a number of other European countries, including France, Belgium and the Netherlands. Nick continues "Marillion, of all people… the post-Fish years."

Is there anyone you would like to collaborate with?
"To write with, it would have to be Bonnie Raitt. 'I Can't Make You Love Me' that is the greatest song ever written. I would like to sing a duet one day with someone like Annie Lennox. I've always wanted to sing with her. Her management company managed us for about a year, and we met Dave [Stewart] all the time but never Annie, only at a gig. She is such a beautiful woman anyway… a beautiful soul, with the great charity work she does, and she's beautiful and she sings like nothing else. So, a duet with Annie… that would be good before I go to my grave."

THEN

NOW

Dear Prudence

Our straight-talking agony aunt, Prudence Prioux, answers your 80's problems with her unique blend of empathy, candor and gothic darkness.

You're So Vain

Dear Prudence,
I am 17 years old and a good-looking guy, but I can't get a girl. I wear the shiniest Sta-Press trousers I can find, the latest Pringle tops, trendy tasselled loafers with bright white towelling socks, and have an expensive corkscrew perm, but I still can't get a girlfriend. All my mates, who don't put nearly as much effort into making sure they look good, are going out with someone. What's wrong with me?

Hugh Jego

Dear Hugh,
I will let you into a secret. No girl likes a boy who spends longer getting ready than she does. Instead of spending all your money on your image, try spending it on the object of your affections. If you are that worried about what you look like, take her somewhere like The Batcave, where the lighting is dark and the clothes even darker. Alternatively, invest in a full-length mirror, and you will be able to see the love of your life whenever you want.

Prudence.

Miss You Like Crazy

Dear Prudence,
Three weeks ago the fair came to town. I met Jack, who is 17, the same age as me, and works on the Waltzer. We met up every day for a week, until the fair moved on. He put me in a spin in more ways than one, and now I can't stop thinking about him. Jack couldn't leave me any contact details as he is always on the move. He said he would write or call me but I haven't heard from him yet. I miss him so much, and don't know how I can wait for a whole year to see him again, when the fair returns.

Lizzy D'Issy

Dear Lizzy,
Sometimes the truth hurts, but Jack has taken you for a ride. As you read this, he probably is having all the fun of the fair with another unsuspecting girl, who has fallen for his nomadic charms. Using his fairground attraction, Jack has played hoopla with your heart and led you on a merry-go-round. In future, when you meet boys like him you need to dodgem, as such encounters are more likely to end in the House of Fun than the Tunnel of Love.

Prudence

Friends Will Be Friends

Dear Prudence,
I met my friend Lisa at primary school and we have been best friends for seven years. We share each other's clothes (I am wearing her batwing top and fingerless gloves as I write this), spend hours together practising our make-up techniques (Lisa has my Bon Bon lipstick on today) and we have even been away on holiday, when my parents took us to Skegness for a week last summer. I can't imagine life without Lisa but there is something that is threatening to ruin our friendship. I am the world's biggest Spandau Ballet fan and plan to marry Tony Hadley (swoon!) when I am old enough. Recently, Lisa announced that she is a big fan of Duran Duran and says she 'loves' John Taylor. I have tried talking sense into her, and play my 'Parade' album whenever she comes to my house, but I can't make her see the error of her ways. How can I be best friends with a Duranie?

Antonia Headley

Dear Antonia,
Instead of looking at your situation as a problem, you need it see it as a gift. As Lisa is such a big Duran Duran fan, she will not be fazed by Spandau Ballet's presence at your wedding. Undistracted by Steve Norman blowing his sax or Martin Kemp looking pretty, she will make the perfect maid of honour. To Cut A Long Story Short she could be your Lifeline, so stop being so Highly Strung and appreciate that True friends like Lisa are pure Gold.

Prudence.

Dear Prudence

Too Nice To Talk To

Dear Prudence,
I hope you don't mind a boy writing to you but I don't know who else to turn to. I find it impossible to talk to girls. Whenever I try to speak to the opposite sex, I blush, struggle to look them in the eye, and stutter because I'm so nervous. I want to ask a girl in my class to come with me to the end-of-term school disco, but I know she will just think I'm an idiot when I try to talk to her and can't get out what I want to say.

Shyboy Shy

Dear Shyboy,
If talking to this girl is such a huge obstacle, you need to find an alternative means of getting your message across. You seem to a sensitive soul, so why not write her a poem asking her out? If poetry is not your thing, you could always 'borrow' some song lyrics to let her know how you feel. My friend Bobby has written some good stuff:
"Yesterday I got so scared, I shivered like a child. Yesterday away from you, it froze me deep inside."
Your other option is to take ownership of your predicament and accentuate your reactions. Deliberately avoid eye contact unless it is to give a look of disdain, keep your head bowed low and occasionally mutter the odd incoherent word. Fans of Matt Dillon and Judd Nelson will be falling over themselves to date you.

Prudence.

I've Got A Crush On You

Dear Prudence,
I am a 15-year-old girl in love with my best friend's brother, Steve, who is 19. Last weekend we were both at his mum's birthday party, and he bought me an Archer's and lemonade. Steve winked and said "don't tell anyone" as he handed me the glass, so I think he likes me too. I didn't get to dance with him because he had brought a date to the party. She has big, permed hair, highlighted with too much Sun-In, and she is a shop assistant in SNOB. I don't think she is very clever and she giggles a lot. Should I tell Steve how I feel?

Judy Judge

Dear Judy,
Under no circumstances should you tell Steve what you think you are feeling. He has shown no interest in you, other than treating his little sister's friend as a 'grown-up'. He likes the woman he brought to the party, even if you don't. Although it may seem otherwise, what you are experiencing is an infatuation which will eventually pass. Until then, you should channel your angst and jealousy into the written word. Heaven knows, if Morrissey hadn't felt as miserable as you do now, most of The Smiths' songs would never have been written.

Prudence

Communication Let Me Down

Dear Prudence,
I am 16 and I am in big trouble with my parents. I wanted to go to a Culture Club gig but there was no public transport running late enough to get me home. I wanted to go so badly that I lied to my parents, and told them my friend Steph had arranged for her older sister to pick us up in her Mini Metro, when it was actually my boyfriend Mark who was going to drive us home. I had not told Mum and Dad about him as he comes from what they would call a 'bad family'. Mark's Ford Cortina broke down when he was meant to collect us, but Steph and I had no way of knowing what had happened. We waited for almost 2 hours for him, before deciding to 'phone my dad and confess. We only had cash on us and, by the time we found a 'phone that wasn't vandalised or accepted only phonecards, it was gone 2am before I spoke to Dad, who came to get us straight away. Since then, he has hardly spoken to me and I have been grounded for a month. How do I make things okay again?

Anna Key

Dear Anna,
Other than hearing "I'm not angry, just disappointed", there is nothing worse than receiving the silent treatment from our parents. Both your mum and dad are having to deal with the fact that you lied, hid your boyfriend from them and put yourself in danger. Your dad is also having to face the truth that his little girl is growing up. I assume you said sorry for what you did, but as an extra apology why not make your dad a mixed tape of his favourite songs? You could even add Feargal Sharkey's 'Listen To Your Father' and Cliff Richard's 'Daddy's Home' to it. Be helpful around the house, do your chores and tidy your room without being asked. Alternatively, you could do what I would have done at your age: return the silent treatment, dress head to foot in black, and rarely venture from the sanctity of your bedroom, where you listen to bands like The Sisters of Mercy and The Damned in candlelit darkness.

Prudence

QUIZZING TIMES

Let's see if New Musik were right when they told us we were Living By Numbers. Use your knowledge of 80's music to solve the following sums.

1	Echo & The Bunnymen's seas	**+**	Stars for the Pearson family	**=**	**?**
2	Double A side with Little Red Corvette	**-**	Year Radio 1 began broadcasting	**=**	**?**
3	Heaven for Glenn Gregory & Co.	**+**	Wonders for Patsy Kensit	**=**	**?**
4	Bryan Adams' summer	**-**	Guns for The Alarm	**=**	**?**
5	Janet Jackson's Rhythm Nation	**+**	Ultravox UK No.1 singles	**=**	**?**
6	Hearts for Phil Collins	**X**	Members in The Kane Gang	**=**	**?**
7	Miles in the title of The Proclaimers' 1988 single	**÷**	Haircuts for Nick Heyward's band	**=**	**?**
8	Bob Marley's little birds	**X**	Goombay Dance Band's tears	**=**	**?**
9	Sweet for Billy Idol	**÷**	Members in Bucks Fizz	**=**	**?**
10	Frankie Goes To Hollywood's tribes	**X**	Hull's score on 1986 Housemartins' album	**=**	**?**

Answers at back of book

20 QUESTIONS WITH
NEVILLE STAPLE

1. What is your favourite 80's song?
'Bankrobber' by the Clash. I have always loved the Clash, plus Bob Marley's 'Redemption Song'.

2. What was the best thing about the Eighties?
Our single 'Ghost Town's' success at a time when the lyrics told a story of the real life. Even though there was one of the biggest weddings of the century (Charles and Diana), real life was bleak, depressed and harsh for everyday people. We hit a raw nerve. How cool was that? So, the best thing about the 1980s, especially the early 80s, was that songs had defining messages that related to real life... not songs for twerking!

3. And the worst?
Margaret Thatcher's Britain and harsh reforms. This led to extensive protests and violent riots. The people felt they weren't heard, so the only outlet for their desperation was to kick out at the system.

4. Who was your teenage crush?
I never had one. I was too busy being rude! Hehe!

5. What was your favourite subject at school?
Playing rugby.

6. What job would you have done if you hadn't gone into music?
I had always wanted to join the Merchant Navy.

7. Who are your musical influences?
Prince Buster, Desmond Dekker, Rico Rodriguez and Stranger Cole. These are all legendary artists from Jamaica whose music has touched the world in one way or another.

8. What was the first single you ever bought?
I bought Desmond Dekker's 'Israelites' and Toots and the Maytals' 'Monkey Man' at the same time in 1969. I already had a huge collection of ska prior to that but I didn't actually buy them.

9. Where did you perform your first gig?
In a band (The Specials) my first gigs were on tour with the Clash in 1978. However, I had done many years of performing (toasting shows) prior to that with my 'Jah Baddis' and with the 'Messenger' Sound Systems.

10. Which five people, living or dead, would you perform with to make the ultimate super group?
Amy Winehouse, Joe Strummer, Sly & Robbie, Rico Rodriguez and my wife Christine Sugary Staple.

11. Who is the most famous person you have ever met?
There's so many to be honest so if I just mention those who are household names now, it would be Pete Waterman, Will-I-Am, Sting, Amy Winehouse, Desmond Tutu, Desmond Dekker, Jeremy Kyle … to name but a few.

12. Which pet hate would you consign to Room 101?
Being man-handled by drunks, and unruly undisciplined pet dogs.

13. What makes you angry?
People with bad manners, especially those who knock you and don't apologise or push past without saying 'excuse me', or don't say 'thank you'.

14. What is the last film you saw?
Close Range (2015) on TV.

15. What are you most proud of?
There have been lots of amazing highlights in my life and career, but right now I am very proud of my latest albums: the double album 'Return Of Judge Roughneck & Dub Specials', where I had the freedom to play with some old ska and reggae favourites, as well as write some new material. Plus, the joint album I produced with my wife Christine Sugary, which will follow. These both have some of my best work.

16. What would be your perfect day?
Relaxing somewhere hot with my wife Christine Sugary Staple, with nice virgin cocktails, sushi or Indian food, couple's massages and spa treatments.

17. What is the best Christmas present you have ever had?
I don't really do Christmas but flying out to Jamaica at Christmas time to get married to my wife, up in the mountains of Christiana (my birth place) was brilliant!

18. And the worst?
All Christmas gifts would be the worst for me really, as I just don't do Christmas. Those who do get me stuff would never know if I hated it, as I always show gratitude.

19. What do you want for Christmas this year?
Nothing. My wife and family will disappear again to be honest, so we don't have to get involved in all the commercial chaos!

20. What are your hopes for the future?
To continue doing live music tours and recording/producing music for myself and others.

Backstage with Christine Sugary Staple

Interviewing Neville Staple at the Looe Music Festival

35

80'S TV AND FILM CROSSWORD

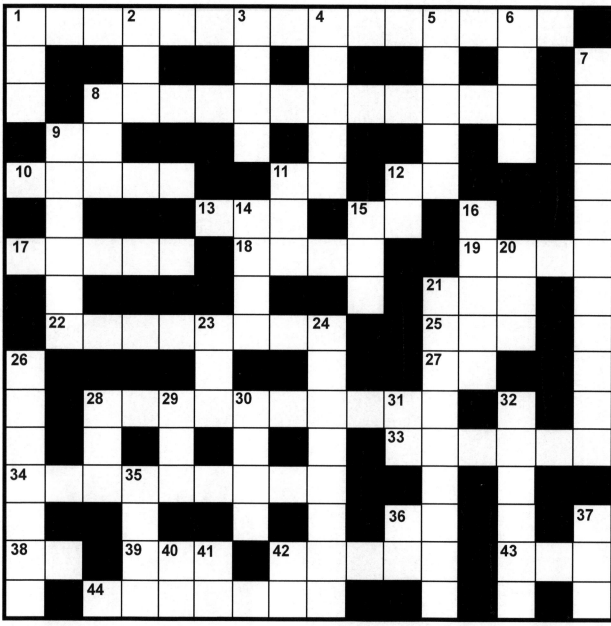

Answers at back of book

ACROSS

1 Sitcom featuring 14 down, 22 across as Vincent Pinner (4, 4, 7)

8 Detective series featuring Bruce Willis and Cybill Shepherd (12)

9 Initially, he was at Heartbreak Ridge in 1986 (1, 1)

10 Mr Lloyd-Pack played Trigger in 1 across (5)

11 Initially, Robert was a Raging Bull (1, 1)

12 Initially, she presented The Tube with Jools Holland (1, 1)

13 Did Christopher Lambert copy his co-stars in this 1984 film? (3)

15 Initially, he followed Phillip Schofield in the 'Broom Cupboard' (1, 1)

17 See 3 down

18 and **26** down Coronation Street character killed by a tram in 1989 (4, 7)

19 These boys included Jason Patric and Kiefer Sutherland (4)

21 Mr Owen played Ricky Butcher in EastEnders (3)

22 See 14 down

25 See 3 down

27 Initially, he began presenting Family Fortunes in 1987 (1, 1)

28 See 24 down

33 Prizes on Big Break were determined by the snooker balls' _____ (6)

34 Alexis Colby married him in Dynasty (3, 6)

36 In brief, this Elmo had a fire in 1985 (2)

38 Initially, she starred with 39 across in Cocktail (1,1)

39 Mr Cruise appeared as Maverick in Top Gun (3)

42 Peter Bowles, James Bolam and Christopher Strauli only did this in hospital (5)

43 Rod Hull's feathery companion (3)

44 See 21 down

DOWN

1 and **4** down He sang the theme tune to Auf Wiedersehen Pet (3, 5)

2 Three Up, ___ Down was a sitcom featuring Lysette Anthony (3)

3 and **17** across, **25** across, **32** down John Sullivan sitcom set in Peckham (4, 5, 3, 6)

4 See 1 down

5 First name of the daughter of 10 across (5)

6 EastEnders' Roly and Willy (4)

7 Series featuring David Hasselhoff and his talking car, KITT (6, 5)

8 Ms Ryan was in Innerspace in 1987 (3)

9 1985 film in which Don Ameche and Jessica Tandy are rejuvenated by an alien life force (6)

11 In short, David Jason's character in 3 down (3)

12 Rank of Reg Hollis and Tony Stamp in The Bill (2)

14 and **22** across He played the lead role in 1 across (4, 8)

15 Which way 9 across can? (3)

16 and **35** down Matchmaking show presented by Cilla Black (5, 4)

20 and **23** down, **37** down Quiz show presented by Paul Daniels between 1982 and 1985 (3, 3, 3)

21 and **44** across Quiz show presented by Nicholas Parsons (4, 2, 3, 7)

23 See 20 down

24 and **28** across Weekend shopping for Mike Read and Sarah Greene? (7, 10)

26 See 18 across

28 The Cosby Show featured this many people in the Huxtable family (3)

29 In brief, the rank of Goldie Hawn's Benjamin (3)

30 Roland and his rodent mates (4)

31 Initially, he was dead in the first episode of EastEnders (1, 1)

32 See 3 down

35 See 16 down

36 Initially, he starred in 9 down and Police Academy (1, 1)

37 See 20 down

40 The heat was here for Glenn Frey's soundtrack to Beverly Hills Cop (2)

41 In brief, the state where Dirk Benedict was born (2)

42 Initially, she appeared as Maggie in Shine On Harvey Moon (1, 1)

Look out for Look-in

In 1980 I was ten years old and completely obsessed with television, so Look-in magazine was my bible. Originally billed as 'The Junior TV Times,' it was way more exciting than that sounds. A riot of colourful TV and pop picture strips, posters, interviews, information, competitions and fun, although because of the TV Times connection any mention of the BBC was right out. This was back when ITV was cool, sort of.

There was, of course, no internet in the Eighties, so where else was I going to be able to read about heroes like Mork and Mindy or Danger Mouse? Reading Look-in now is a fascinating exercise in nostalgia for me. When I see a glossy cover image of The Kids From Fame or Bucks Fizz, it takes me right back to my crazy childhood, when nothing was more important than watching Tiswas or listening to The Human League, often at the same time. I miss some of that passion, misguided though it may have been, but the world of TV and pop was incredibly exciting for a kid living in the middle-of-nowhere (Penn in Buckinghamshire, if you must know).

Tiswas was the highlight of my week. Chris Tarrant's torrent of insane comedy sketches, silly competitions and custard pies completely captivated me as a child. The show never talked down to its audience, something which I subconsciously appreciated. It came from Birmingham, but to me it might as well have come from the moon, so little did we travel as a family, and so little did I know about the world. I hungrily devoured any morsel of information I could find about the show, and when a weekly Look-in page was given over to Tiswas I couldn't have been happier. It was only a few photos and the odd snippet about Spit The Dog, but to me it was manna sent from Birmingham.

My parents viewed this fascination with all things television as a form of madness which, in a way, I suppose it was. They strictly limited the amount I could watch, but this made me even worse, and my weekly appointment with Look-in became even more precious. Benny Hill was definitely frowned upon. Now, I can see why, but I loved him at the time and was able to follow his adventures in comic strip form thanks to the land of la-la-la-la-la-Look-in.

Cannon and Ball had their own picture strip entitled, unsurprisingly, 'Rock On Tommy'. Although they are almost forgotten now, at the time, their ratings eclipsed even those of the all-conquering Morecambe and Wise. I thoroughly enjoyed the Madness picture strip, which was full of superbly surreal Nutty Boy lunacy, and was great fun to read, mostly due to the larger-than-life characters in the band. The Haircut 100 strip was less successful. Apart from Nick Heyward, who had ever heard of any of them? Their stories appeared "by arrangement with Haircut 100" which I'm glad was made clear.

As the Eighties progressed, the magazine dropped the beautiful painted covers to make way for photos. Instead of TV stars they started to feature more pop people, but it was such an exciting time for music that all this was fine by me. One week you would have Altered Images, the next week Duran Duran. All flamboyant, colourful, upbeat pop fun. Sometimes they would combine TV and pop in a wonderful way. I remember a pull-out poster of Debbie Harry in a girl-guide outfit, surrounded by The Muppets, with the lyrics of 'Rapture' thrown in for good measure. Ah, the Eighties! With the addition of Look-in Profiles, one could discover that Tracey Ullman's favourite food was twiglets, or that David Hasselhoff had five cats and two parrots. Today, every kid's magazine seems to come with at least twenty free gifts, but in the Eighties the prospect of a free smurf sticker was something to look forward to. At least it was in my case. As I say, we didn't go out much.

Let's look at a typical issue of Look-In. How about 6th June, 1981? First of all, I am struck by the amount of material packed into it, and the sheer quality of the artwork. It has a big painted cover of Jon and Ponch, the two 'daring' motorcycle cops from CHiPs, a hit TV show about the California Highway Patrol. Inside there is a CHiPs interview, poster, comic strip, and even a potato-themed recipe. That show must have been popular! It was, of course, a massive success all over the world, except in my house. I have to admit that I used to turn it off after the cheesy but catchy theme tune.

Leafing through the magazine further reveals a feature on Russ Abbot's Madhouse, a big Saturday night sketch show that even my parents didn't mind watching. Abbot's more memorable characters included teddy boy Vince Prince, secret agent Basildon Bond, and my absolute favourite, Cooperman: Russ as Tommy Cooper as Superman. Do you see what they did there? The whole show combined silliness with quick-fire gags and loony goings-on. A winning combination as far as I was concerned.

Next in this particular issue, we come to a competition in which readers can win... wait for it... a £3.00 postal order. It might not seem like much, but this was back in 1981, when £3.00 bought you half a Rubik's cube. There is a fabulous picture strip of Buck Rogers In The 25th Century, which practically leaps out of the magazine, with some stunning space-age artwork and peculiar alien characters. The strip seems to have lasted a lot better than the actual TV show, weighed down as it was by Bacofoil spacesuits and hammy acting. There is also a Spot The Difference section, featuring two not-quite-identical photos from the dimly remembered Popeye film with Robin Williams. I went to see it at the time and found the whole thing incomprehensible. Now, it is another happy Eighties memory.

In the middle of the magazine comes the pièce de résistance: a colour centre on Spandau Ballet. This is a rather grand term for an interview and a poster. However, important quotes and lyrics from the band abound, with Gary Kemp saying of his songwriting "Words are used more for their sound than their meaning". That explains a lot. Screen Quiz is up next, and here is a question from it to test your Eighties' knowledge. Who was the main presenter of Tyne Tees TV pop

show Razzmatazz? Sadly, there are no prizes as our budget doesn't run to £3.00 postal orders, but you can find the answer at the foot of the page.

There is lots more pop and TV action throughout the issue, which comes to a close with a preview of next week's issue, starring Adam Ant on the cover. That is nothing unusual but, for some reason, there is also the promise of a feature on The Bermuda Triangle. The Bermuda Triangle? You've lost me there!

Looking back, Look-in really did give its young readers a lot to la-la-la-la-la-look at, and to quote from the TV Times advert of the day, I never knew there was so much in it! Now, let's get the smurf out of here ...

Follow John on Twitter: @johndredge

Answer: Alastair Pirrie.

80'S SPORT WORDSEARCH

```
A L X N D C B B O B R I A N J A C K S H
W S O N D H H J K R K I B A A H O C T I
E T D H U A S S T E F F I G R A F T E G
H F A L B D R B T E S S I I F F O F V S
D F L L A S J A K O I T S U G F A R O E
O I E I L H A R K Y P T X G U T L A V R
O V Y V O A C R V V O H E C I R E N E N
G G T R Z R K N J P R S O M N U X K T O
N T H O B R I A H O T H A Y K S H B U S
A E O T A O J E H E E W O R S H I R X R
C F M E R N R D V A H A T R T T G U K E
N F P N R D S E U I O R E A E O G N A D
U I S Y E A O O T N M K V B J N I O D N
D T O A W V N B S P C J R E D X N O A A
V A N J E I R J Y E N O O A D I S N L S
P F P T G E K C B O R A T N U A L C Y A
O X T R A S T S U Z A N N K B N B K T S
T E U D X H I G G N S A R F O R O S H S
Y L U S R R G O O H E W D D X U I A M E
M A O S O D N A D E N N A Z U S K A S T
I A N B O T H A M M N U A F F H E O N J
```

Alex Higgins	Barry McGuigan	Boris Becker
Brian Jacks	Christopher Dean	Daley Thompson
Duncan Goodhew	Fatima Whitbread	Frank Bruno
Ian Botham	Ian Rush	Jayne Torvill
Sharron Davies	Steffi Graf	Steve Ovett
Suzanne Dando	Tessa Sanderson	Zola Budd

Growing Up With Jamie Days

Monday 24th September, 1984
At lunchtime we can stay inside and read in the hall. I got sent out because I didn't have a book.
Tamsin is reading Adrian Mole and she was showing me where there are rude parts in it. We sat on the crash mat.

Wednesday 26th September
Day was a drag. I am reading the Secret Diary of Adrian Mole now. Mum wasn't sure if I should be allowed to read it but Dad said it was okay. I mean big wow I know it all already! Sally was crying on the way home. She told me and Emma that Becky and Faye were sat behind her today and were sticking a compass in her and pulling her hair. I feel dead sorry for her.

Saturday 29th September
I read Adrian Mole. He is painting his Noddy wallpaper black.

Sunday 30th September
Asked Dad if I can paint over my Perishers wallpaper. He said no and Mum started making a right fuss going on about it had to last. In Adrian Mole it says joss sticks are drugs. Sean had some of them when he went camping!!

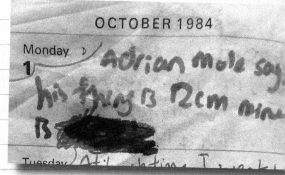

Monday 1st October
Adrian Mole says his thing is 12cm mine is [entry obscured by violent crossing out].

Sunday 7th October
Sean has tuned my radio into Radio One so I can listen to the Top 40. Ghostbusters is no.2. Watched It'll Be Alright on the Night. Adrian Mole has got swollen nipples. That better not happen to me!

Monday 8th October
Asked my dad what a wet dream was. Not that I don't already know. He started giggling. It was dead funny. Nearly burst out laughing but managed to hold it in. Wait 'til I tell Alistair.

Saturday 13th October

Had to go to Skipton with Mum and Dad.
It was boring. Saw the new Adrian Mole
book. I want it. Got me some pick n mix
in Woolworths.

Sunday 21st October

In Tenko there were naked women in the
bath together. You got to see their tits but
they weren't that impressive.

Sunday 4th November

Me and Vicky went out for mischief night.
We did 'knock and run' and garden hop-
ping. I got right from Emma's down to The
Willows! Reet doss! My mum and dad got
me the new Adrian Mole book instead of
having fireworks. Can't wait to read it.

Tuesday 6th November

I don't fancy Vicky any more but I still
fancy Claire and Lynsey. In Adrian Mole
Pandora dumped him because he asked to
see her tit. I would like to touch
someone's tits.

Thursday 8th November

In Integrated Studies Angela was trying to
get everyone to get her to ask people out
for them. I didn't join in because I fancy
Lynsey but she is too old for me. Adrian
Mole's thing is 14cm now but his mates
comes off the end of a ruler!

Monday 12th November

I was off school because I was sick in the
night. It was boring but better than school.
Adrian Mole had a wet dream because he
read about sex and reproduction. He is
such a moron.

Growing Up With Jamie Days

Friday 23rd November
At lunchtime Justin hid Martin's pencil case. He was going bright red trying to find it. It was funny until Sarah grassed. It was Children in Need tonight. It was so boring, I came to bed and finished Adrian Mole. It's dead good.

Sunday 25th November
Listened to the Top 40 and there is a song called 'Sex Crime 1984'. That's Deon, that is!

Friday 30th November
Deon was on about sex again. He said there's a thing called a mars bar party where you put a fun size mars bar up the woman and the man licks it out. We went round all the girls asking if they'd ever had a fun sized mars bar!

Monday 3rd December
Last night I was sort of playing with my thing when I thought I was going to wee. I ran to the bathroom but instead of wee a little bit of white foamy stuff came out. I was about to shout Dad when I realised what had happened.

Sunday 9th December
Just tried that thing again I did last Sunday night. There was more stuff this time and it was better. I put the stuff on the carpet. If anyone ever reads this I'll die!

Sunday 10th February 1985
Today was pretty boring. David came round and we played Donkey Kong on the computer. Dad wanted to look at my wobbly tooth but I wouldn't open my mouth. He was crazed.
P.S. Dad just came in and asked me if I know what the stains are on the carpet! I said I didn't know and that I wondered that too. I was so embarrassed but I managed to cover it up. I wonder if he saw me when he was in the garden and I was in the lounge and put it under the hearth rug! He better not have!

Friday 26th April

Dad just came in to my room and talked about wanking. He said there are two types of men: those who admit they do it and those who lie, and that I shouldn't worry about it. I just don't want them to know that I'm doing it.

Thursday 9th May

Had the day off as NUTS on strike again. Emma's sister Claire came round so Sean could help her with some homework. She said Marc Almond collapsed on stage and when they pumped his stomach they found a pound of another man's spunk in there. It's the most disgusting thing I have ever heard.

Thursday 30th May

It was really hot today. I have made a secret den by the reservoir by pulling away some of the fencing. No one can see me in there. I have agreed to start wearing deodorant today. I smelt my armpits this morning and they stink. I noticed a smell but didn't realise it was me. I can't be bothered having showers all the time. It is Sure roll-on and it's blue. Top of the Pops was dead good. I like 'Duel', and might buy it.

Saturday 29th June

Went to town and met Alistair. We both bought the 'Paisley Park' single. We talked about the sex education books. His brother found his and his mum got him done for it. I read all of mine last night. We walked down to look at the hairdresser that has a Durex sign in the window. We are really good friends now.

Friday 5th July

Today in Science we did the male reproductive system. Mr Dunn said the man does about a teaspoon full of sperm. You must do less when you get older. He also said his favourite word is epididymis. Wally asked what happens if the man accidentally urinates in the woman during sex. He's such an idiot. We can stay behind afterwards and ask him questions if we want. I am going to when I can think of one.

Tuesday 23rd July

Went round to Katie and Vicky's. We were in their back garden talking about getting greasy skin. Their mum said it's because of puberty, then she said we are all pubes!

Saturday 5th October

The Blue Lagoon was on tonight but I wasn't allowed to watch it so after I'd gone to bed I snook down and sat on the stairs and watched it through the lounge door. I saw her get her period in a pool and then a bit where he was wanking behind a rock but there were no other rude bits I saw.

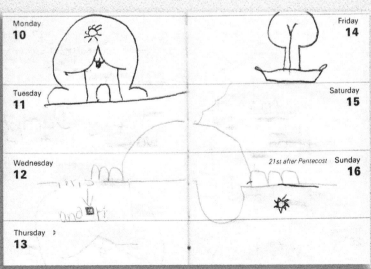

POP QUIZ

compiled by Alan Read

Q1. What name is shared by the different groups who had hits with 'Yes Tonight Josephine' in 1981 and 'Crush On You' in 1987?

Q2. 'Dream Into Action' was the second album by which solo artist, released in 1985?

Q3. "We sit and watch umbrellas fly" is the opening line from which A-ha hit?

Q4. Who presented the Radio 1 chart show between 1984 and 1986?

Q5. Robert Palmer, Maxi Priest and Rod Stewart all had hits in the 80s with different versions of which song?

Q6. Break Machine had 3 hits in 1984. "Street Dance" and "Are You Ready" were two - what was the third?

Q7. What was David Bowie's first hit of the 1980s?

Q8. 'Leather Jackets', '21 at 33' and 'Breaking Hearts' were all Eighties' albums by which legendary artist?

Q9. Who co-wrote and produced 'Each Time You Break My Heart' for Nick Kamen?

Q10. Horace Panter, Roddy Radiation and Lynval Golding were members of which group? The Specials

Q11. What was 5 Star's highest charting single?

Q12. How many UK number 1 singles did Wham! have?

Q13. What was the name of the band formed by Mick Jones after leaving The Clash?

Q14. Who did Alexander O'Neal duet with on 'Saturday Love'?

Q15. How many number 1 albums did Phil Collins have in the 1980s, as a solo artist and as a member of Genesis: 7, 8 or 9?

Q16. What was Nick Heyward's first solo hit single?

Q17. In the lyrics of 'Alphabet Street' where was Prince going to drive her?

Q18. The Thompson Twins' Tom Bailey and Alannah Currie wrote which 1989 hit for Deborah Harry?

Q19. What was The Smiths first Top 10 hit of the 80s?

Q20. The Police were the only act to achieve what UK double twice in the 80s?

Q21. Which UK city did The Specials, King and The Primitives all come from?

Q22. 'Neutron Dance' by Pointer Sisters was on the soundtrack of which Eddie Murphy film?

Q23. Who released the album 'East Side Story' in 1981?

Q24. Who were Andy McCluskey and Paul Humphreys?

Q25. Sheila Hylton had a hit with a cover of which Police song?

Q26. What was the first No.1 single produced by PWL?

Q27. 'I Heard It Through The Grapevine' and 'When A Man Loves A Woman' were both used to advertise which product?

Q28. Between 1987 and 1989, how many singles were released from Michael Jackson's 'Bad' album?

Q29. Michael J. Mullins and Geoff Deane were both lead singer of which band during the 80s?

Q30. What do S'express, Talk Talk and Visage have in common?

Answers at back of book

47

BACK TO SCHOOL
WITH LEE MACDONALD

At the age of 12, Lee MacDonald landed the part of Samuel 'Zammo' McGuire in the BBC children's hit TV series Grange Hill, and appeared on our television screens for the first time in 1982. Four years after his arrival at the fictional North London school, Zammo became the central figure in the show's most memorable and highly publicised storyline, which saw an ordinary teenage schoolboy begin his decline into heroin addiction. Lee recalls some of his memories of that time.

What do you remember about your first day on set?
My first day on set was when we filmed the episode at Chessington Zoo. It was an amazing day. All the episodes were filmed out of sequence because we filmed all the location shots first. This episode is my all-time favourite.

Who were your best friends at Grange Hill in real life?
I was friends with all the cast, although Erkan [Mustafa, who played Roland Browning] is the one I keep in contact with most. We all keep in contact through Facebook, and meet up from time to time.

What was it like appearing on Pointless with Erkan?
I have appeared with Erkan twice on Pointless, and both times have been great fun. Me and Erkan have a great relationship on and off screen. We are doing a big Children In Need gig later this year.

Do you have any funny stories from your time on Grange Hill?
Turning the lights off in the BBC changing rooms and having 'hanger throwing' fights. Also, we were in the next changing room from the guys in The Young Ones, and we used to drive them mad by knocking on their door then running away!

What do you remember about your visit to the White House as part of the Just Say No campaign?
This was a massive part of my life and I have such fond memories of our visit to the White House to meet Nancy Reagan. We also had a Top 5 UK single,

which for anyone is amazing, but at 16 was unreal. We toured America with our single and sang at the Yankee Stadium in front of 80,000 people.

What were your thoughts when you first discovered Zammo was going to get involved in drugs?
It was a big decision for me and my family to agree to do this as I had to do lots of research with real drug addicts, but Anthony Minghella [the show's script editor] made sure I was comfortable with everything. I am so glad I went ahead with the storyline. It had such a big impact at the time, and still does.

Did you feel any pressure playing the key character in such an important storyline?
No. I was only 15 or 16 at the time, so you take it all

You haven't turned your back on acting completely, so is there anything in the pipeline?
I own Mentor Lock in Wallington, Surrey. That keeps me busy but I still work in films and TV. I have just finished Two Pigeons, which was directed by Dominic Bridges. I am now with a new agent, Cherry Parker, who has some exciting plans for me. So, who knows? Maybe Eastenders in the future!

Following your departure from Grange Hill, you had planned to take your amateur boxing to the next level. However, any plans to turn professional were scuppered by a motor collision when you were 21. Are you still a fan of boxing despite no longer being able to fight?
No, once my boxing career was stopped due to my car accident, I did not really follow boxing. That said, I loved to watch Mike Tyson in action.

Is there anything you miss about the Eighties?
I miss the clothes and music from the Eighties, especially my Fila and Sergio Tacchini tracksuits.

What was your worst fashion mistake during the Eighties?
Bleached jeans with frayed hems.

What is your favourite song from the Eighties?
Looking For That Perfect Beat by Afrika Bambaataa.

And favourite film?
I have two. *Ferris Bueller's Day Off* and *Back To The Future*.

If you could travel back to the Eighties, what advice would you give your teenage self?
Wow, that is a tough one! I would say use the money you earn wisely by investing in property, because the years go so quickly you need to be prepared for your later years.

in your stride. I was so comfortable with Zammo's character, I was prepared for anything Zammo was asked to do.

What research did you do to help you play a heroin addict?
At the time, I was not aware of the drug heroin, so it had a big impact on me. I watched various videos of drug addicts, given to me by the BBC. I also visited various rehabilitation centres to meet and chat with addicts.

How did being in Grange Hill impact on your personal life?
Grange Hill had a massive impact on my personal life at the time because it regularly had viewing figures of 9 to 12 million, so everywhere I went I would get recognised. I did love it though as a teenage boy. It was great with the girls!

You have hardly changed since we used to watch you in Grange Hill. How does it feel to still be recognised as the character you played more than three decades ago?
I love it when people chat to me about Grange Hill now as I had such fun filming it. Also, it had such a big part in people's lives at the time. Everyone I meet and chat to about Grange Hill has very happy memories of the show.

What are your thoughts on being a child actor? What are the advantages and disadvantages?
The advantage of being a child actor is it gives you a great start into the business, but if you stay in a role too long you can get typecast, which can be very negative.

Me with Lee in 2013

RESPONSIBLE RADIO

During the Eighties, it was not only children's television programmes wh[ich] aimed to educate the nation's youth in the danger of drugs. The "number c[ne] station" BBC Radio 1 used its far-reaching broadcasting influence to laur[ch] its Drug Alert campaign in 1987. Based on information from the Institute [for] the Study of Drug Dependence and written by Plain English Campaign, t[he] booklets, "A Guide To The Effects and Dangers of Drugs" and "How To G[et] Help", accompanied the station's on-air coverage.

Considering the target audience was teenagers, the booklets make interesting reading, offering a glimpse of the decade's adolescents, how they compare to the current generation of teens, and one of the approaches used to address the issue of drug use. Including content more suited to primary school children, there is a page entitled "What the jargon means", defining terms such as "tolerance", "withdrawal effects", "dependence" and "addiction", the first booklet also offers advice, some of which may now be considered questionable, on the dangers of drug taking, including tobacco and alcohol. The guide goes on to classify drugs as Heroin and Other Opiates, Cocaine, Solvents, Amphetamines and Other Stimulants, Cannabis, LSD, Hallucinogenic Mushrooms, Hypnosedatives and Minor Tranquillisers, and looks at their legal status, availability, long and short-terms effects.

The second booklet provides an outline of the same drugs, followed by practical advice on how to quit them – "You've already achieved it by picking up this booklet" – including counselling services, treatment, self-help and community groups. In today's age of instant information, courtesy of the internet, these publications provide a fascinating insight of a bygone era's response to an ongoing problem. However, I am still uncertain whether "Most drug offences are not discovered. But to help enforce drug laws police have very wide powers. For instance, just planning together to commit a drug offence leaves people open to the same sentence they might have got if they'd done it" would have terrified teenagers from even thinking about drug use or encouraged them to partake, as they were going to receive the same punishment regardless of actual participation.

The following excerpts show more of the information and advice we were given in the booklets:

"All drugs can be dangerous in some way, but only some are illegal. Tobacco and alcohol, which are widely available and legally, contribute to the death of about 107,000 people a year in Britain. The illegal use of heroin and cocaine kills about 280. But if heroin and cocaine were as easily available as tobacco and alcohol, they would probably be major killers as well."

"This guide does not look at why some people misuse drugs, nor why some drugs are illegal and some are not. The answers to these questions lie in the history and culture of this country — not just in the drugs themselves."

"Regular use of cocaine is still limited to the wealthier part of the population. However, its use is spreading … Tolerance does not necessarily develop. Users are often tempted to step up the dose because of the feelings of physical and mental well-being produced by the drug."

"Solvent misuse seems to become common in a small area (say an estate or a school), mainly among youngsters aged 12 to 16. Then it may quickly disappear … Accidental death or injury can happen because sniffers are 'drunk', especially if they are sniffing in an unsafe place such as on a roof or by a canal bank."

"Tolerance and dependence are likely to develop to any sedative. The dependence has a strong bodily (as well as mental) basis."

"About a third of children between 13 and 16 years of age drink at least once a week, mostly in the home and in small amounts. Relative to wages, the 'price of a pint' dropped by half between 1950 and 1982."

"Many people who smoke regularly say they find it relaxing and yet stimulating at the same time, and get great satisfaction from inhaling."

"In people who have developed bodily dependence and tolerance to opiates, pleasure is replaced by the relief of getting the drug. They need it just to stay 'normal' … Bodily dependence is not as important as the strong mental dependence developed by some long-term users. Dependence of any kind is not inevitable."

"There is no proof that cannabis use over a long time causes lasting damage to bodily or mental health. This may be because the kinds of study needed to detect slow-to-develop and uncommon results have not been done."

"Most people who have tried drugs have come to no harm. But most drugs have side-effects that can be dangerous if users don't know what they're doing or use drugs regularly or mix them. Most of this guide is about the dangers."

"As with other calming drugs, people who often get 'high' on cannabis may appear apathetic and dull and neglect their appearance etc, but there is no evidence that cannabis destroys people's motivation to work."

"As with LSD, tolerance rapidly develops. After using for a few days, no matter how many mushrooms are taken, the user will not recreate the experience. This discourages frequent use."

"Tranquillisers depress mental activity and alertness, but don't generally make people as drowsy or as clumsy as the barbiturates … On their own, tranquillisers rarely produce the feeling of happiness that come[s] with barbiturates or alcohol."

"About a quarter of 14-15 year olds smoke at least a cigarette a week. Among older teenagers about 30% smoke, each consuming on average 11-12 cigarettes a day."

RADIO 1 DJS OF THE 80S

On 30th September 2017, BBC Radio 1 celebrated 50 years of broadcasting across the nation's airwaves. For many of us growing up in the Eighties, the station and its DJs became synonymous with the music of our youth. Here, Richard M. White takes a look back at the DJs who brought us the tunes that made our memories of the decade.

SIMON BATES

Simon was the only permanent fixture in the Radio 1 daytime schedule during the whole decade. He was actually heard on weekday mornings for 16 years between 1977 and 1993; his most well-known features were The Golden Hour, Our Tune and The Birthday File. He also hosted two Tuesday night phone-in current affairs shows, starting in 1980 with Personal Call. He came back to the slot in October 1982 with Frontline, which ran until September the following year.

Bates returned to the Top 40 for the first nine months of 1984, having previously presented the chart between April 1978 and August 1979. He secured many exclusive interviews with the likes of Wham!, Spandau Ballet, Madonna and Tina Turner, and also questioned the leaders of the three main political parties prior to the 1987 General Election. Simon's most ambitious project came in the summer of 1989 when he travelled around the world with his producer Jonathan Ruffle, which he admitted he dreamed up to avoid doing the Roadshow.

TONY BLACKBURN

Tony opened up Radio 1 in 1967 with Flowers In The Rain by the Move, and it was also the last record he played before leaving the network 17 years later. In January 1980, he succeeded Ed Stewart on the children's weekend request show Junior Choice on Saturday and Sunday mornings, as well as continuing on the Top 40. He presented a record 123 consecutive chart shows from 2nd September 1979 to 3rd January 1982, during

which time he added two million listeners and won Best Radio Show of 1981 in the Smash Hits readers' poll. His mispronunciation of a new group "Durran Durran" earlier that year remains his best remembered chart moment. Two months later, the Junior Choice name was discontinued with the weekend programme being rebranded as Tony Blackburn's Saturday/Sunday Show. It continued until his departure on 23rd September 1984.

JAKKI BRAMBLES

Jakki arrived from London's Capital Radio in the summer of 1989 at the age of 22. She first appeared as a member of Simon Mayo's breakfast crew before debuting on the weekend early show (5-7am) on 1st July. After filling in for various colleagues over the summer, she graduated the equivalent weekday slot (albeit only a 90 minute show) three months later, following the departure of Adrian John. She was the first female DJ to broadcast regularly in the daytime schedule, and made her debut appearance of Top Of The Pops alongside Bruno Brookes just 12 days after presenting her first show. Brambles later hosted the drivetime and lunchtime shows before leaving the station in 1993.

BRUNO BROOKES

The DJ formerly known as Trevor Neil Brookes first appeared on Radio 1 in the summer of 1980, at the start of a nine week experiment in which various BBC local radio presenters were given the opportunity to host the evening show from 8pm. The first person to appear in this slot was billed as Bruno of Radio Stoke. It would be another three and a half years before he would return to the station, initially sitting in on Steve Wright's then Sunday morning show. He took over the teatime show from Peter Powell in September 1984, and succeeded Richard Skinner on the Top 40 on 30th March 1986. Bruno moved permanently to the weekend breakfast show in April 1989, co-hosting with Liz Kershaw in a partnership that had actually begun three months earlier. He ended the decade on a high, being voted best DJ of 1988 and 1989 in the Smash Hits readers' poll.

PAUL BURNETT

Paul began the decade hosting the lunchtime show between 11.30am and 2pm, where he had resided since the summer of 1976. His popular features included Fun At One, in which he played a daily comedy clip, Pub Of The Day, and Juke Box Junction, described in Radio Times as "a country classic for those on the move". For many listeners, his important job of the week was revealing the new Top 40 on a Tuesday at 12.45pm. He would reveal the top five in reverse order, then give a full chart rundown, shortly before one o'clock and playing the number one. He featured the new entries and climbers in the remaining hour of his programme. In October 1981, he was shifted to a later slot between 2 and 3.30pm where he stayed until April 1982. After a few months hosting a Saturday morning show, Paul left the station in October for a brief spell at Radio 2.

GARY BYRD

The longest Top 40 hit single of the decade, The Crown, which clocked in at 10 minutes 35 seconds, was performed by a man whose appearances on Radio 1 spanned just over three years. He presented a Sunday night neo-gospel show, Sweet Inspirations, for just over a year from 11th March 1984, featuring artists such as "Thomas Dorsey, Mahalia Jackson, James Cleveland and Shirley Caesar" who were all name checked in the show's introduction. Gary was heard on daytime Radio 1 in early 1985 for two weeks when he stood in for Steve Wright. He took over the American chart show on 15th February 1986 from Paul Gambaccini, for whom he had once deputised in December 1983. While Gambo only ever featured the Billboard Top 30, his successor extended it to the Top 40 and also revealed it a full week before its official publication date. The show later switched its chart source to the rival Radio and Records list, with Byrd's final appearance coming on 10th January 1987.

NICKY CAMPBELL

The only DJ to have a jingle that spoke his full name, Nicholas Andrew Argyle Campbell, arrived at Radio 1 from London's Capital Radio in October 1987. He initially presented on Saturday nights between 10pm and midnight, before moving to the weekend early show. He deputised on all the daytime shows before an extension in Radio 1's broadcasting hours saw him promoted to a new daily late night slot on 3rd October 1988. Initially airing between 10.30pm and 12.30am, it featured regular live sessions and special guests and ran for an impressive five years. Nicky made his debut on the Radio 1 Roadshow in 1989, the same year he presented a three part series called Let's Spend The Night Together, which saw him interview all the members of the Rolling Stones.

GARY DAVIES

The self styled "Medallion Man" joined Radio 1 in December 1982 for a Saturday night show that aired between 10pm and midnight, with the first record he played being Layla by Derek and the Dominos. He graduated to lunchtimes on 25th March 1984, where he remained for nearly eight years. Gary was the last regular DJ to "reveal" the new chart on a Tuesday. For his rundown backing music, he used an instrumental version of Prince's 1999, which was specially edited by his then producer Kevin Howlett. Adopting Sunfire's Young Free and Single as his theme song during his early days at the station, Gary could also be regarded as the George Lazenby of the Top 40. He presented the station's Sunday flagship chart show just once in the Eighties, deputising for Bruno Brookes on 6th September 1987.

NOEL EDMONDS

Between 1973 and 1978, Noel presented the Radio 1 breakfast show, but by the Eighties he was presenting his innovative Sunday morning show, which included his imaginative world of funny 'phone calls, misheard lyrics and fictional places like Dingley Dell and Perkins Grange. The show attracted a high calibre of guests, including Denis Healey, Geoffrey Howe and Harry Chapin. It was originally co-hosted by famous war time announcer John Snagge, before Radio 4 announcer Brian Perkins took over. Edmonds left Radio 1 in 1983, but made a brief comeback in February 1985 when he stood in for Mike Read on the breakfast show, and featured in the Radio Radio documentary series the following year.

Noel also enjoyed chart success as the drummer on the Brown Sauce single I Wanna Be A Winner. The record, which peaked at number 15, was recorded with Keith Chegwin and Maggie Philbin, his co-hosts on Multi-Coloured Swap Shop, the Saturday morning children's show that ended its six year run on BBC 1 in 1982.

ALAN FREEMAN

"Fluff" returned to Radio 1 after an 11 year hiatus in January 1989 with a revival of both his Saturday Rock Show and Pick Of The Pops, which returned to the BBC as an "oldies" show for the first time. It featured Top 20 charts from three different years in a two and a half hour show, during which he played the complete Top 10 and a selection of songs from numbers 20 to 11. Unlike the present incarnation of the show on Radio 2, the countdowns played before February 1969 were the BBC own charts, which were compiled by averaging out the positions from the various chart music papers of the day (these were used on the original POTP shows on both the BBC Light Programme and the early days of Radio 1, which differed from those adopted later by the old Guinness Book of British Hit Singles). Fluff's POTP run on Radio 1 lasted until the end of 1992 but continued with the Rock Show for another nine months. After a spell back in commercial radio, he returned to the BBC in 1997 for another four years at Radio 2. He passed away on 27th November 2006, aged 79.

PAUL GAMBACCINI

The "Professor of Pop" is best remembered at Radio 1 for his Saturday afternoon American chart show, which ran for more than a decade until 8th February 1986, when he joined Capital Radio in London. Paul also appeared as a regular guest on Roundtable, a Friday night show which reviewed the new single releases. He also hosted it for three months in the summer of 1980, during which time he filled in on the teatime show for two weeks after the departure of David Jensen.

During 1981 and 1982, he presented an Appreciation series of documentaries, celebrating legendary pop and rock figures from the previous 30 years, with further new episodes being aired in 1984. Paul was one of six subjects chosen for the 1986 Radio Radio documentary series, which celebrated the work of innovative DJs from the station's history. He returned to Radio 1 for a second three year spell in 1991.

MARK GOODIER

Mark made his Radio 1 debut on Boxing Day 1987, in the same slot Gary Davies had begun five years earlier, between 10pm and midnight on Saturdays. He quickly became the regular stand-in presenter on the Top 40, first sitting in for Bruno Brookes on 21st February 1988. He deputised on the chart show on nine occasions in the last two years of the Eighties, before having two spells as main host from 1990-92 and 1995 to 2002. His first public appearance with the station came on 2nd May 1988, when he co-hosted a Teddy Bears Picnic Roadshow from Chatsworth House, Derbyshire with Mike Read and Peter Powell, whilst continuing to fill in on various daytime and weekend shows.

On 1st September 1988, Goodier co-hosted the first Top Of The Pops to be simulcast as part of the opening phase of the station's big stereo switch-on to full time FM broadcasting. A month later, he moved to the weekend breakfast show, which he co-hosted with Liz Kershaw. He took over the teatime show the following April, where he remained until the end of the decade.

DAVID JENSEN

"The Kid" began hosting the weekday afternoon show between 4.30 and 7pm in 1978, and was still in that position as the new decade dawned. He left Radio 1 in June 1980 to join Ted Turner's new cable television station, TBS (Turner Broadcasting System, now CNN) in Atlanta, Georgia to co-host a nightly news programme. He returned just over a year later, on 4th October 1981, to the 8 to 10pm evening show, where he remained until the summer of 1984, before signing for London's Capital Radio. David initially hosted a mid-morning programme and later the Network Chart Show, which was commercial radio's rival to Radio 1's flagship Top 40 on Sunday afternoons. This chart was also seen on television in June 1987, when Jensen helped launch The Roxy. This was billed as ITV's alternative to Top Of The Pops, but the show was axed after just 10 months.

ADRIAN JOHN

Adrian was the king of early mornings on Radio 1 for the most of the decade, taking over the 6-7am slot from Mike Smith in April 1983. His trademark laidback style had first been heard three months earlier when he began a weekly Saturday show, 6 to 8am, which he continued until the end of September that year. Between March and September 1984, he presented the early show from Mondays to Thursdays, and a Friday afternoon programme, whilst also deputising for Mike Read at breakfast for four weeks that summer.

John was on the presenting roster for the Radio 1 Roadshow every year between 1985 and 1989. In May 1986, his early show was extended to 90 minutes, starting at 5.30am. Later that summer he was part of the presenting team that covered Prince Andrew and Sarah Ferguson's royal wedding. Adrian left the station in September 1989.

Adrian Juste and Adrian John in 2016

ADRIAN JUSTE

Adrian's winning combination of various classic comedy clips, along with his own puns and short sketches between music tracks, were heard on Radio 1's weekend schedules for more than 15 years. These intricately produced clips included the likes of Fawlty Towers, Tony Hancock and Carry On films, and were sometimes edited into one sequence.

His best remembered time slot was 1 to 2pm on Saturday lunchtimes, where he resided from 11th November 1978 to 28th March 1981 (barring a two month break in 1980), October 1981 to April 1983 and, finally, from 5th October 1985 to 1st January 1994. Juste was also heard on Sundays, initially for six months in 1981 and later for two years from September 1983, firstly between 10am and 12 noon, and then in a later 90 minute afternoon slot from 2.30 to 4pm. He also hosted many Bank Holiday and New Year's Eve specials and provided numerous voiceovers, including trailers and DJ introductions for the Radio 1 Roadshow.

JANICE LONG

Janice's five year tenure at Radio 1 began on the same day as Gary Davies (4th December 1982) with a new Saturday evening show between 7.30 and 10pm. Her show included news from the Northern music scene and weekly sessions featuring acts like Aztec Camera, Fiat Lux and A Flock of Seagulls. It ran until 22nd September 1984, by which time she had moved to weekday evenings, where she remained until the end of 1987.

Janice had two spells hosting the Friday afternoon show Select A Disc, in which listeners could choose their favourite Top 40 hit, in 1984 and 1985, and in May 1986 she was chosen to host Singled Out, a revival of the old Roundtable format. As well her involvement with Live Aid and the 1986 Royal Wedding, Janice also hosted special programmes from Tokyo and Moscow and interviewed hundreds of stars, including Paul McCartney, Eurythmics and Rod Stewart.

SIMON MAYO

Simon arrived at Radio 1 from BBC Radio Nottingham in March 1986, and was first heard deputising for Gary Davies on the lunchtime show for two weeks. His first regular show, which aired on Saturday nights between 7.30 and 10pm, ran from May 1986 to September 1987. This was the same time slot Simon occupied for the first four months of 1988, when he was moved into the weekday schedule, following a brief spell on the weekend early show.

On 23rd May 1988, he took over the Breakfast Show and introduced a "zoo" format with newsreader Rod Mackenzie and Sybil Ruscoe, who read out the travel and weather headlines. She was later succeeded in the role by Carol Dooley, Jakki Brambles and Dianne Oxberry. During his first two years on the network, Mayo also hosted Radio Scruples (a celebrity game show) in late 1987 and the inter-schools pop quiz, Pop Of The Form in early 1988, with both shows going out on Sunday afternoons.

ANNIE NIGHTINGALE

Radio 1's first female DJ will forever be associated with her Sunday night Request Show, which ran for 12 years from December 1982. It initially aired between 8-10pm, before moving an hour earlier to immediately follow the Top 40, in April 1983. However, at the start of the Eighties, Annie was presenting two weekly shows. On Wednesday evenings she hosted Radio 1 Mailbag, which answered listeners' letters on almost any subject, while her Friday night show, which ran until 2nd October 1981, saw her residing over an eclectic range of music and features. She continued with the former show until its demise in September 1983. As well as being the only UK broadcaster at Live Aid Philadelphia, Nightingale also presented a number of documentaries. These included a 20th anniversary celebration of the Beatles' Sgt Pepper album, Rock In Russia, which reflected on her visit to the Soviet Union in 1987, and a two part special on Simple Minds in 1989. Annie joined Radio 1 in 1970 and remains there to this day.

MARK PAGE

The DJ that referred to himself as "Me Mark Page" enjoyed four years on Radio 1, mainly hosting the weekend early show which he began presenting on 1st October 1983. He also appeared on Fridays for 18 months from March 1984, firstly in his familiar early slot and later in the afternoons, a show he presented for a year until October 1985. Mark was the quizmaster for two series of the Sunday afternoon celebrity based The Great Rock 'n' Roll Trivia Quiz in 1985 and 1986. His other projects for the station included a six part documentary series, City To City, a tour of the UK's musical hubs from Liverpool to Newcastle. Mark continued with his weekend commitments until he left the station in September 1987.

ANDY PEEBLES

During his 13 years at the station, Andy presented in every single time slot, from the breakfast show to the Top 40. He began the decade hosting a weekday afternoon programme and a Thursday night pop current affairs show Talkabout, which he left in June 1980. The same month he took over the agony aunt/uncle style Monday night programme Stayin' Alive, which he co-hosted with Dr Alan Maryon Davis and Alison Rice until the end of 1982. He moved to a weekday morning show in September 1980 before launching his Friday night music and sport show in October 1981. Six years later, he moved to Sunday nights to host Andy Peebles' Soul Train, which reverted to Saturdays in April 1989. As well as narrating numerous documentaries, Andy hosted the long running series My Top Twelve (later My Top Ten), interviewing an eclectic range of stars, from Phil Collins to Ian Botham and Martin Shaw, who selected their all-time favourite tracks. However, Peebles will be forever remembered for his interview with John Lennon, which took place in New York two days before the former Beatle's death on 8th December 1980. He left Radio 1 in February 1992 and retired from broadcasting in March 2014.

JOHN PEEL

John Robert Parker Ravenscroft, better known as John Peel, was the longest serving DJ of the original BBC Radio 1 line-up. He broadcast regularly from the station's launch in 1967 until his death aged 65, on 25th October 2004. The show always featured sessions from two bands that were generally very big in the independent charts but still awaiting their mainstream breakthrough. The exceptions to the rule were bands Peel picked up on first and followed throughout their careers. His programme never followed a set format, featuring everything from obscure African music, rock 'n' roll classics to avant-garde European electronic music and punk. His annual Festive 50, which started in 1976, counted down his listeners' favourite tracks from the previous 12 months. Such was Peel's reputation into breaking unsigned acts into the mainstream, he would receive dozens of demo tapes every week.

In October 1987, he made a six part series, Peeling Back The Years, where he talked to his long-time producer, John Walters, about his listening life. He followed this in March 1988 with John Peel in Russia, where he visited Moscow and Leningrad talking to young Russians about their own listening tastes and lifestyles. His numerous accolades and awards included winning the Sony award for National DJ of the year in 1986, and being awarded an OBE in 1998.

PETER POWELL

Peter moved into the daytime schedule in September 1980, having previously hosted a weekly Saturday morning programme between 10am and 1pm. He took over the teatime show, which initially aired from 3.30pm to 6.30pm, having deputised in the slot a month earlier that summer. From 1981, he was mainly heard between 4.30 and 7pm. Features included The Record Race, where a listener could win up to 10 singles, depending how quickly they identified the intro to a record, and 5 45s at 5.45, a daily spot where five new singles were played. Peter reviewed the new singles chart on a Tuesday and album chart on Thursdays, which moved to Wednesdays in late 1982. He also featured sessions by up and coming acts, including Spandau Ballet and Duran Duran. On 29th September 1984, Powell moved to the weekend breakfast show, which he presented until 25th September 1988, when he left radio altogether to concentrate on his talent management company, James Grant Media.

MIKE READ

Mike was Radio 1's longest serving breakfast show host in the Eighties, waking up the nation for more than five years between January 1981 and April 1986. Regular features included Schooldesk, First Love and Beat The Jock, along with a review of the new singles chart on Wednesday mornings. He had already deputised at breakfast for six weeks in the summer of 1980, a year which saw him mainly presenting the evening show at 8pm. For the first nine months of 1981, he hosted Roundtable, a role he would return to six years later under the show's retitled name of Singled Out. In May 1986, he moved to Sundays between 10am and 12.30pm, and in October 1987, he could be heard between 10pm and 1am on Saturdays, and on a new two hour Sunday oldies show at 1pm. Mike also hosted two Sunday afternoon shows, Pop Of The Form, in 1987, 1989 and 1990, and two series of The Chart Quiz in 1988 and 1989, which featured top pop personalities. His oldies show moved to an hour long Monday night slot in 1989 and was renamed the Mike Read Collection. Read's many special projects included a 50th anniversary celebration of Abbey Road studios in 1982, a Wham! Christmas special in 1985, and an eight part series McCartney on McCartney in 1989.

PHILLIP SCHOFIELD

Phillip made his debut on the station in 1988, when he presented a two hour August Bank Holiday special between 8 and 10pm, having first come to prominence on television three years earlier when he became the first in-vision continuity announcer for Children's BBC. In October, he began hosting Going Live on Radio 1, a Sunday afternoon magazine style show with music, guests and competitions which ran alongside an hour long request show on Thursday evenings. He occasionally stood in for Simon Mayo on the breakfast shows, and was the first compere of the Smash Hits' Poll Winners Party, which also launched in 1988.

ROGER SCOTT

Roger rejoined Radio 1 in July 1988 after nearly 15 years at London's Capital Radio, having presented some shows for the network in the early 1970s under the pseudonym of Bob Baker. He took over The Stereo Sequence on Saturday afternoons from Johnnie Walker, before being given a second show Scott on Sunday, which aired from 11pm to 2am, three months later. He also devised the series Classic Albums series, in which he interviewed an artist or band and played tracks from their career-defining album. Roger made his last broadcast on 8th October 1989 before sadly losing his battle with cancer at the end of that month. He was 46 years old.

Four days later, Radio 1 broadcast a special 90 minute tribute as part of their Radio Radio series, in which Roger talked about his fascinating life and career. He was later celebrated at a special star-studded memorial service at Abbey Road, part of which was broadcast on 23rd December 1989.

PAT SHARP

"Patman" is probably best known for his 10 year stint at London's Capital Radio, starting in 1987, but had a brief spell at Radio 1 in the early part of the decade. He was first heard on the station in September 1982, when he sat in for a week for Steve Wright and began hosting the new early show on Sundays between 6 and 8am three months later. He hosted Top Of The Pops on three occasions in 1983, before leaving the station at the end of September to move into commercial radio, initially at Radio Mercury. In 1988 and 1989, he had two Top 20 hits with his Capital colleague, Mick Brown, with charity covers of Let's All Chant and I Haven't Stopped Dancin' Yet. They reached number 11 and 9 respectively, and raised thousands for Capital's annual Help A London Child appeal.

RICHARD SKINNER

Richard reverted to full time music presenting at Radio 1 at the start of 1981, after seven years as one of the main presenters of Newsbeat. He presented the Monday to Thursday 8 to 10pm evening show for nine months, having hosted the teatime show for six weeks during the summer of 1980. In October, he began a four year stint as the host of Roundtable, and in January 1982 replaced Tommy Vance on the Saturday afternoon magazine show Rock On (renamed Saturday Live in April 1983).

Skinner presented the Top 40 show between 30th September 1984 and 23rd March 1986, and played a major role in the BBC's Live Aid coverage in 1985, beginning with his opening announcement: "It's 12 noon in London and 7am in Philadelphia". After spending two and a half years at London's Capital Radio, he returned in October 1988, initially to host a new daily late night show and a major documentary series The Beeb's Lost Beatles Tapes. He later took over The Saturday Sequence after Roger Scott's untimely death, before leaving the station for good in 1991.

MIKE SMITH

Mike had two short spells at Radio 1 in the Eighties, having worked at the station as a freelance producer/presenter from 1975. After four years at London's Capital Radio, his "on air" return came on 1st October 1982, when he appeared as part of that week's review panel on Roundtable, before sitting in for Peter Powell on the teatime show the following week. He soon began a Saturday morning show which aired from 10am to 1pm, a role that continued when he became the station's first presenter of the weekday early show in December. In April 1983, he took over the lunchtime show for a year before moving into television, becoming part of the on-air team on BBC1's Breakfast Time.

Smith returned in May 1986, when he took over the breakfast show from Mike Read, going on to win the Smash Hits best DJ award for 1986 and 1987. He left the station exactly two years later, and sadly passed away on 1st August 2014, aged 59.

DAVE LEE TRAVIS

"The Hairy Cornflake" was the third DJ to present the Radio 1 breakfast show, from 2nd May 1978 to 2nd January 1981. He then moved to a daily afternoon slot of 2.30 to 4.30pm, where he remained for nearly nine months. During this period, he also presented a Thursday night programme Wheels, which featured everything from hot rods and trains to roller discos, motorcycles and cars.
In October 1981, Travis replaced Paul Burnett on the lunchtime show. As well as unveiling the new chart on a Tuesday, his other regular features included 12 O'Clock Rock and a mystery voice competition called Replay. His weekly three hour Saturday show began in April 1983, before he moved to Sunday mornings in October 1987. A year later he was on both Saturdays and Sundays, where he remained until his famous on-air resignation in August 1993. Dave is perhaps best remembered for his innovative quizzes, Give Us A Break ("snooker on the radio") and his inter pub darts contest Treble Top.

Pat Sharp in 2017

DAVE LEE TRAVIS

TOMMY VANCE

Tommy was born Richard Anthony Crispian Francis Prew Hope-Weston, in 1940. His Friday Rock Show, which ran for 15 years from November 1978, was one of only a handful of programmes to run on Radio 1 throughout the whole of the 1980s. In 1980 and 1981, he presented Rock On Saturday, which, according to its Radio Times billing, featured "music, news, interviews and more music, with full coverage of the national and international rock scene". He left the show to take over the Top 40, which he presented for two years from 10th January 1982 to 1st January 1984.

Vance also hosted Into The Music, which featured a mainly AOR playlist, on Thursday nights for almost a year from 4th October 1984, and Night Rockin' at midnight on Saturdays, for three months from October 1988. Tommy also introduced many special programmes, including a Status Quo 20th anniversary celebration with Francis Rossi and Rick Parfitt in 1982, and an overview of the 1989 Moscow Music Peace Festival. He died on 6th March 2005, aged 64.

ROBBIE VINCENT

After presenting two series of hour long Saturday soul shows on Radio 1 in 1977 and 1978, Robbie returned to the station in 1982, when he had a three month spell as chairman on the Tuesday night discussion show Talkabout. His new Sunday night show began in January 1984, in which he played the best in soul, funk, jazz and fusion. One of its best remembered features was Music For A Candlelit Dinner where he would play a segue of four or five romantic soul tracks. Regular listeners will instantly recall Robbie's spoken jingle "If It Moves – Funk It"

The show later included star interviews and live concerts from acts such as Maze and Anita Baker. Robbie moved to Saturday nights in October 1987, where he stayed until he left Radio 1 at the end of 1989, a year that also saw him present The Godfather of Soul, a three part documentary series about James Brown.

JOHNNIE WALKER

Johnnie returned to Radio 1 after an 11 year absence in January 1987, presenting a new five hour Saturday strand, The Stereo Sequence. It included documentaries, features, a new look American chart show with Laura Gross "plus music on album and compact disc" as per its billing in Radio Times. His second spell at the station lasted only 18 months, but shortly before his departure at the end of June 1988, he was the main anchor of Radio 1's coverage of the Nelson Mandela birthday concert from Wembley Stadium. After a brief stint at The Superstation, Richard Branson's syndicated service which provided overnight programming to several ILR stations, Walker returned to the BBC in October. He was part of the original on-air line up at the BBC's new local station, Greater London Radio (GLR), where he remained for the rest of the decade. His final spell at Radio 1 came between 1991 and 1995.

STEVE WRIGHT

Steve made his Radio 1 bow on the opening weekend of 1980, hosting on Saturday nights between 7.30 and 10pm for three months. He moved to weekend mornings in June, firstly on Sundays and then Saturdays from the end of August until October 1981, by which time he had moved into the daytime schedule. Steve Wright In The Afternoon initially ran from 3.30 to 5pm, before it was extended to 2 to 4.30pm in April 1982. It included characters such as Mr Angry from Purley, Dave Doubledecks, Gervais the Hairdresser, Happening Boy and Damian the Social Worker, who were played by his production team, the Afternoon Boys. One of the show's catchphrases, I'm Alright, was turned into a novelty single which reached number 40 in December 1982.

In October 1984, the show's start time moved back to 2.30pm, and then 3pm a year later, where it remained for the rest of the decade. Between October 1983 and April 1986, Steve was moved from Fridays to Sundays, firstly in the afternoons from 2 to 4pm, and then in September 1984 from 10am to 12.30pm. In 1982, Steve was the regular film contributor to the Monday evening show Stayin' Alive, and in 1988, he hosted Celluloid Rock, a six part series which covered 30 years of rock in the cinema.

He was voted best DJ of 1985 in the annual Smash Hits readers' poll.

There were numerous other on-air DJs who played their part in Radio 1's success story, maintaining the station's position as "The Nation's Favourite" during the Eighties. These included: Graham Bannerman, Andy Batten-Foster, Madeline Bell, Ian Brass, Peter Clayton, Stuart Colman, Pete Drummond, Mark Ellen, Laura Gross, Annemarie Grey, Stuart Grundy, Bob Harris, Lenny Henry, Paul Jordan, Phil Kennedy, Andy Kershaw, Liz Kershaw, Alexis Korner, Adrian Love, Al Matthews, The Ranking Miss P, Ro Newton, Dixie Peach, Emperor Rosko, David Rider, Jimmy Savile, Tim Smith, Pete Tong, John Walters, Jeff Young.

Richard M. White is a journalist, writer, researcher and well known radio chart show archivist. He runs @classiccharts on Twitter and Facebook, which features daily tracks and trivia from the two hour era of the Top 40 show from 1978-1990.

JUST A FEW QUESTIONS FOR ADRIAN...

Occupying the Saturday lunchtime slot for most of the Eighties, Adrian Juste was an integral part of Radio 1's successful formula, which saw the station riding a wave of popularity during the decade.

Many people who listened to Radio 1 as a teenager in the 1980s would consider it to be a golden age of radio. Would you agree?
It certainly was if you were a Radio 1 DJ. Management took a back seat and left us to it. Ideas and energy weren't strangled at birth as they are now, and eccentricities and personal traits were encouraged at every turn. Witness Steve Wright's enormous success of the period. By the middle of the decade, Radio 1 was pulling in a weekly audience of around 24 million. The Roadshow was proving a highly successful ambassador for the BBC, underlining its national status, and the new soap EastEnders had huge figures. This left the suits to concentrate on Radio 3, Glyndebourne and all the worthy stuff which justified the corporation's 'unique & prestigious' tag. Everyone was happy.

What are your memories of your time presenting the Saturday lunchtime show on Radio 1 in the Eighties?
Well, it was hard work! [I had] very little social life outside the BBC, and I lost

a couple of nice girlfriends because the network demanded total dedication, and the life was anything but a 'normal' one. I did make a few quid on the many disco gigs, and moved from Kettering to a nice big place in Gerrards Cross, where we built a lovely new multi-track studio. Radio 1 tried me in a couple of different time slots during the Eighties, which I didn't really settle in, but when Johnny Beerling was appointed controller he restored me to that 1 o'clock Saturday spot, and it all worked again.

Your shows were an intricate mix of comedy and music. How long would it take you to put together each week's show? Did you ever worry you would run out of ideas?
Only for the first 6 weeks! As we were all in uncharted waters in Spring '78, we just didn't know. But we soon got into a rhythm of doing comedy clips, impersonations (especially of Alan Freeman) and throwing a bit of production around old jokes. I soon settled down into more writing and went trawling for American comedy discs, a real rarity in those days. I also spent a lot of time in the BBC Gramophone Library, which proved a rich vein of obscure stuff. There was always new material to go at, which sparked off ideas. I'm still friends with a couple of Gram Library staff to this day. They and their knowledge proved invaluable. The actual show took a good 3½ days each week to produce, with a lot of thinking time on top of that.

What was it like being part of the Radio 1 'family' during the Eighties? Was it as much fun as it appeared to be to us listeners?
It certainly was. Because we were all so busy with gigs, OBs [outside broadcasts], Top of The Pops, etc., we didn't see too much of each other. So, like a successful marriage, a bit of distance never goes amiss! We had good executive producers who could handle us artistic types and any ego problems, but not many arose. They were very good at heading off any potential issues. We finally moved out of Broadcasting House and into our custom-built studios on the second floor of Egton in the mid-Eighties, to become completely self-contained. We even lived above the Gram Library - very handy!

Have you stayed in touch with your former Radio 1 colleagues? Which fellow DJs were your friends in 'real life'?
With one or two exceptions, we all stayed in touch. And on the rare occasions we meet up at functions, the years just roll away, and we pick up exactly where we left off. DLT and wife Marianne were great friends... many lovely showbiz parties at their old place... and we're still friends now. I still see Andy Peebles and Mike Read, who's invariably bobbing about in Henley. There's the very funny Paul Burnett and his wife, Nicole, and I bumped into Tony Blackburn in Regent Street not so long back too. I also still see many of the old producers, who were great and really knew

how to coax the best performance from their 'turns'. I also got to know John Peel quite well ... always good to meet your heroes.

The DJ cull instigated by Matthew Bannister in 1993 has been well-documented. To what extent do you feel his actions were a knee-jerk reaction to the growth of commercial radio?
Commercial radio didn't have too much to do with it. It was more the Tory government waging war on the BBC, as usual. Never listening to the network, they didn't understand that what we were doing was musically different from super-safe ILR [Independent Local Radio]. Birt [former Director General of the BBC, John Birt] appointed Bannister to make the station distinctly different, which he duly did ... gifting the commercial concerns 9 million listeners in the process. No conspiracy though, just a bunch of people who hadn't a clue what we'd built up and achieved over the years, and didn't care.

To be fair to them though, the political landscape was a minefield at that time. The corporation really needed a stronger DG, like Sir Hugh Carleton Greene in the 1960s, who told Westminster emphatically to leave broadcasting to the broadcasters. Sir Hugh was not a man who rolled over and played dead.

Following that cull, many listeners who felt alienated by Radio 1's new format re-tuned their radios. It could be argued that for a generation of forty-somethings, Radio 2 is now the number one station. What are your thoughts on this?
In 1994, Radio 2 was far from ready to take up the baton. The whole thing was never thought through, and many of the disenfranchised Radio 1 listeners decamped, somewhat grudgingly, to their local commercials. Radio 2 was still all Nat King Cole, Listen To The Band and the Midland Radio Orchestra. Quite enjoyable, but making that jump from Gary Davies and Steve Wright, playing East 17 and Take That, was a quantum leap too far for most folk.

As for the Radio 2 of today, I don't listen myself... any listening now is confined to speech radio or BBC Surrey... but a friend in the village has it on permanently, for her dog! It seems quite noisy, and what is this relentless obsession with TV people? I find the network frustrating, because it could be so much better.

As Radio 1 celebrates its 50th Anniversary, what do you believe is the future of radio?
I haven't got a clue! Let's be honest, 'experts' have been trying kill radio off for decades, but the patient refuses to lie down. The short-term quick profit brigade of the commercial sector are unwittingly doing their damnedest to bring about its demise, but even then it's still remarkably buoyant. I do wish they'd stop their persistent attempts to appeal to the 'yoof' audience. The youngsters aren't interested these days and, thanks to our cash-strapped society, have no disposable income anyway.

Radio could well become something that people 'grow in to', much like one does with Radio 4. As people appreciate the finer things in life and have a little more experience of the world, they'll appreciate the medium more. It'll be a natural progression, and it's futile to try to force the pace.

Can you tell us about some of the main changes in radio you have experienced since you first began your career at Radio 1 in the late Seventies?

Well, two things to sadden the heart, really. The lack of investment by major record labels in new acts and songwriters throughout the Eighties, which has led to a distinctly lack-lustre look to the pop music of the 21st century. They were just content to take the big profits from established bands, plus the highly lucrative re-issue of all their back-catalogue on CD. The other sea-change was when radio studios started to resemble an accountant's office. This enabled the 'suits and skirts' to suddenly feel at home, to poke their noses in, rely on very dodgy focus groups, and display a woeful lack of competence, whilst collecting disproportionately large salaries for screwing it all up. I always loved the epitaph written at the time, which is sadly still waiting, predator-like in the wings: 'Here lies Radio - researched to extinction'.

Imagine you have been given your own radio station to run for the day. How would your dream schedule run? Which DJs would you include?
I won't do the usual list of suspects. Let's take a positive and forward look at things. I'd shop around the UK for a few of the new talented presenters, let them choose the music, tell them to forget everything they've been told by Rex Bob Lowenstein-style advisors. Just go on air, be yourself, enjoy yourself, and let 'em rip! According to your question, it's only for a day so couldn't do any damage, and would probably do an awful lot of good all round!

What do you miss about the Eighties?
I don't miss the British cars! In the death throes of our car industry, they were dreadful and unreliable. We did so many miles back then, and I had many let-downs. I particularly remember missing a TV rehearsal at Hammersmith Palais because of a once-great British marque. Completely disaffected, I then went German, and have stayed German.

I realise the Eighties were difficult for many people in the UK but, speaking purely personally, I was making a nice living and thoroughly enjoying life. But we were working darned hard. I suppose one thing I miss is the preponderance of satirical shows there was back then, the rise and rise of Spitting Image being a particular favourite. There is now no one around to deflate the egos of the many self-important bozos who make our lives such a misery. Everything is so, so serious.

What is the highlight of your time at Radio 1?
Ooh, an impossible choice. So many great memories of my time on 'The Nation's Favourite'. I'll never forget each Saturday, around 3 minutes to air-time, the SM [studio manager] would come down the talkback with those immortal words: 'We're in network'. Then, after whatever sort of week you'd had, whatever financial issues beset you, whoever had upset you, you knew you could forget all of it for 60 minutes. It was showtime! Can I just recall my funniest BBC moment? That's much easier.

In the early Nineties, the show was repeated mid-week, and London control room would record the live broadcast on the Saturday. But one week we suffered from having too many cooks. One department was trusting the other department to record, and vice-versa. The result was they didn't have it, and had to pay me to come in and do the whole show again, live, word for word. Even the great BBC got it wrong just occasionally!

FOR THE VERY FIRST TIME

The first single in our record collection may not always be one that shaped our future music tastes, but it is one we will always remember. Some of our 80's favourites reveal what was the first single they ever bought.

Martyn Ware
"I think it was 'Metal Guru' [by T-Rex]. I can't remember one earlier than that. The thing is, my house was full of vinyl anyway because I've got two older sisters, who had a huge record collection. So, it wasn't like I needed to buy records. We already had a house full of vinyl."

Jay Aston
"'Cinderella Rockefella' by Esther and Abi Ofarim. I don't know why!"

Peter Coyle
"Suzi Quatro 'Devil Gate Drive'. I loved her. Her voice... the way she sings. It's gorgeous, really gorgeous. I think, very underrated, actually. It was hard because she was being a pop artist, but if she could have been more like Janis Joplin. You see, I can't help myself... it's great that she was a major success but if she could have stepped out of that, it could have been so exciting. It was brilliant anyway, and she was good at what she did and I loved her voice."

Jona Lewie
"I didn't buy my first one, because that was a birthday present from my grandma and mother: 'Don't Knock The Rock' by Bill Haley. I bought a couple of Lonnie Donegan seventy eights in 1957... 'Gambling Man' and 'Cumberland Gap'. 'Gambling Man' was Number 1 for seven weeks, and it was a sensational live performance on a Sunday night, at the London Palladium. He was highly influenced by Huddie Ledbetter, who was Lead Belly, a blues singer. I bought those seventy eights and I bought 'She's Got It' by Little Richard. That was my last seventy eight. That was the Christmas of 1957 and, to me, it was a magical year for music. I was so young [Jona was ten]. My first 45 rpm was 'Good Golly Miss Molly' by Little Richard, in 1958."

Cheryl Baker
"Mine was 'Rosie' by Don Partridge. I don't know why. I think it's probably because I had enough pocket money that week to buy a single, so I didn't care what it was, I just wanted to act grown up. But my first album was 'Abbey Road' so I got my credibility back with that!"

Mike Nolan
"The very first record I bought was 'Cracklin' Rosie' by Neil Diamond. He's great."

Bobby McVay
"Donny Osmond 'Puppy Love' and I got two copies of it. I went out and bought it and my sister went and bought it for my birthday."

Eddi Reader
"I stole 'The Wombles of Wimbledon' from Woolworths for my sister's third birthday. We lived on a council estate and we didn't have any money, so that's what I did. My first proper, with my wages, record was 'The Hissing of Summer Lawns' by Joni Mitchell."

David Ball
"It was 'Love Grows (Where My Rosemary Goes)' by Edison Lighthouse, on Bell Records, and the second record I bought, which was dreadful, was 'Back Home' by the England World Cup football squad, 1970, and we didn't win. It had a dreadful B-side called 'Cinnamon Stick' and I still, to this day, cannot figure out what the hell that's got to do with a football team. I even remember who wrote the first single I bought... Tony Macaulay. He was a massively successful songwriter. He wrote hits for David Soul and all sorts. That guy wrote so many hits... he probably had more hits than Stock, Aitken and Waterman. I think he was once on Top of The Pops in three different bands but that was him, Tony Macaulay."

Neville Staple
"You mean nicked?" Neville laughs. "I can't remember," he says, but he can describe how he used to acquire his music collection. "It was Pete Waterman's store. He had a record store. I used to get stuff from Virgin Records as well. There was Virgin Records, and the next floor was Pete Waterman's store, so I used to travel up there then come back down."

Dave Wakeling
"Oh baby, baby, it's a wild world," sings Dave. "On Island Records, the reggae version. No, that's not true. I bought some before then. That was my introduction to my first reggae single. Rolling Stones, '19th Nervous Breakdown'. Who knew that was going to be such a recurrent theme amongst my songs? Great song."

Junior Giscombe
"The Kinks' 'You Really Got Me'. "They were brilliant, The Kinks. I love that band."

Nik Kershaw
"The first single I ever bought was 'Your Song' by Elton John. I just loved that song. My parents had a radiogram, so it was all mono. There would be the odd Mozart piece or Lonnie Donegan they'd play on it. When I first started getting some pocket money and was old enough to get on a bus and go into town on my own, I thought 'right, I'm going down the record shop now to buy that record'. I played it to death.

Nick van Eede
"The original, and much better version than Phil Collins, 'A Groovy Kind Of Love' by The Mindbenders."

Growing Up With Jamie Days

Saturday 22nd September 1984

We went to town. Sean wore his 'I'm With Stupid' t-shirt, but in Marks & Spencers he sat on a chair and you couldn't see the "with" part where it folded up. It was dead funny. Got a blank tape to tape The Empire Strikes Back off Benson.

Saturday 6th October

Got the bus to town and met Bernie. I bought the Ghostbusters single then in Broadbents I saw the Princess Leia figure from the first Star Wars. I rang Dad and asked him to come and pick me up so he could lend me the money. I got it but no damn pocket money for 3 weeks to pay for it. Just my luck.

Thursday 18th October

Alistair is having a Halloween party next week and I am invited and so is everyone else. Mum says I am allowed to go but I am not allowed to trick or treat because it's American and it's begging. I am doing though – no fear!

Wednesday 31st October

We are not allowed to trick or treat so me and Vicky went out as Ghostbusters. I made signs for us from the single cover and we had shaving foam to squirt at any ghosts. I ran past Mazz to squirt her but hit her head with the can. Did trick or treating in secret. Got some spice and £1.74 each. Someone gave us satsumas so we squashed them on their car!

Saturday 15th December

We went Christmas shopping. I got Nana Oil of Ulay, Grandad chocolate gingers, Mum a new mug off the market and Dad the Colemanballs book. Sean bought Nellie the Elephant and he took it to a party tonight even though Dad said not to. We put up the Christmas tree this afternoon.

Wednesday 19th December

Dad lost his temper with me today because I went through the Christmas Radio and TV Times and put a star next to all the programmes I want to watch, which is what he usually does. He says he can't do it now. Big deal.

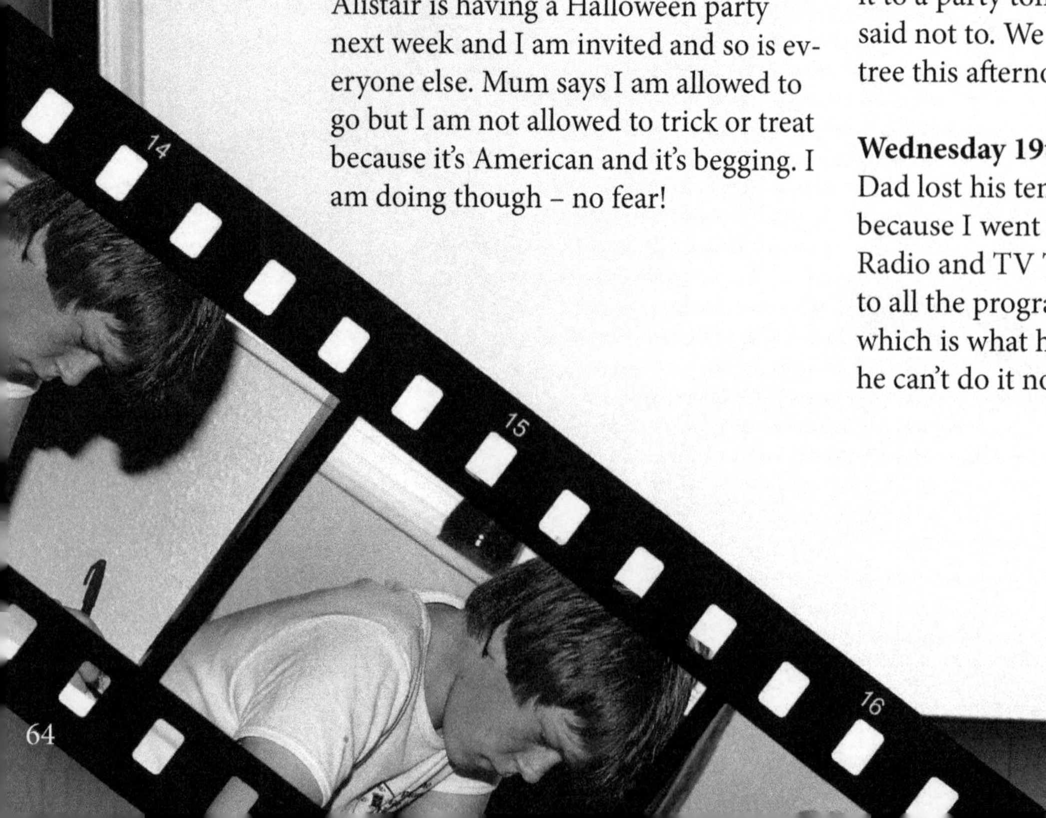

Monday 24th December
Went round to Nikki and Mazz's tonight cos their mum and dad went to the pub. They've got a video and we watched Fame. It was really rude, there's a bit where Leeroy rubs his thing then his bum and then this man makes Coco take her top off. We were giggling like mad. It's really good but not as good as the TV series though. Grandad bought the turkey round.

Thursday 27th December
We went shopping to spend some Christmas money. I bought 'Like A Virgin' by Madonna and 'The Frog Chorus'. I was embarrassed buying a record by a woman in case they think I'm a sissy. I met Mum and Dad in Sparks's and they got me to tell the woman at the till what I bought. I said "The Frog Chorus" and they said "and another one didn't you?". I had to say "Like A Virgin by Madonna" and she shook her head and said "what's the world coming to?". The cheeky cow. I don't know what a virgin is but I know it's bad.

Growing Up With Jamie Days

Wednesday 6th February
Benson came round with 'I Know Him So Well' so we could tape it for Mum. After that I was dancing to 'Teardrops' (and other things on side 4 of my Hits tape) in the lounge, but I felt dizzy because I am still full of cold. Heard mum on the phone to Katie's mum talking about me.

Saturday 16th February
Went to get a new school bag and coat. I wanted a Coca-Cola bag in a can shape but they didn't have any so I had to get just a plain barrel shaped one. It's dark blue but it's padded so looks a bit sissy. The man on the market stall said it was for boys and girls but I'm not sure. I hate my coat too. I wanted a jacket but mum said I have to get one that keeps my back warm, so it's long. Good news is that I got a new diary in the sale at WH Smith for 49p. That's a bit sissy too but I'll put stickers on it, and it reminds me of Strawberry Switchblade. It's not got that much room for each day but there's loads of notes pages in the back.

Wednesday 6th March
On the way home Adam Johnson called me a puff and shouted that my bag was a girl's bag. He said my coat was puffy too. Cathy stuck up for me and told him to piss off. She said she liked my bag but Mel said my coat was a "bum warmer". I am never wearing it again.

Friday 15th March
School was OK today. Science was great. We went outside to draw lichen. but in History we had a test on the Armada. Nick Babb let me copy. Went to James Adams after school and got mum a pot robin for Mother's Day. It was £3.49 so I'm broke now. I stormed upstairs because I can't have my bedroom decorated, only new bedding. I am so mad. I'm sick of the fucking Perishers - it's so babyish! I am going to be 12 for God's sake! Mum was just cross because of something in the paper about the by-pass. They had another meeting. Dad's letter was in it too. I almost smashed the robin on purpose but I didn't.

Tuesday 19th March
It's my birthday tomorrow but I am depressed. I have no proper friends and get picked on at school. I just want to be popular and for people to like me. Apart from that, the day was okay.

Wednesday 20th March
My 12th birthday and it was rubbish except for all the presents I got. I got £5 from Nana and £10 from Auntie C. Auntie Tina sent me a rugby shirt and Auntie Joan gave me a £3 postal order, that mum says has to go in my Post Office account. Mum made a cursing cake* for us all and we had my favourite tea. It snowed a bit too. Not bad I suppose.

Saturday 25th May
Went to see Morons from Outer Space with Nikki and Mazz. It was funny, especially when he sneezed in his space helmet! The usherette was telling us she has a brain haemorrhage and could drop dead at any moment and blood would come out of her eyes, her nose and her mouth. She was scary!

Thursday 15th August
Watched a vampire film called Salem's Lot. It was really good. There was this creepy bit where a boy floats at a window. I am not sleeping with my curtains or window open tonight.

*so called because the recipe was so difficult Mum would always swear when she was making the cake.

Tuesday 24th December
Went down to the village and then into town. Only got £2.30 for my papers last week. Tonight I went to Lisa's party. Spencer was there and Redz. They were putting matches out in drinks because they said it makes you more drunk. I think they were just acting drunk. Mum was mad with me because I was late back and she had made me mince pies and brandy butter, but I didn't really want them. Watched 'Arthur' and then came to bed.

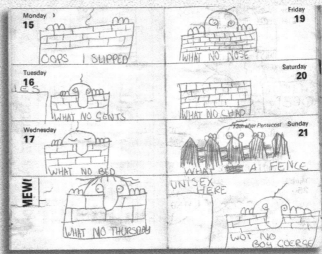

A PIECE OF THE ACTION WITH THE FIZZ

After winning the *Eurovision Song Contest* in 1981 with their future chart-topper 'Making Your Mind Up', Bucks Fizz went on to further UK chart success in the early Eighties with a string of Top 10 hits, including two more number one singles '*The Land Of Make Believe*' and '*My Camera Never Lies*'. The band has seen a number of line up changes and name variations over the last three and a half decades, before reaching its present, and arguably best, formation. Featuring original members Cheryl Baker, Mike Nolan and Jay Aston, alongside Bobby McVay, a former member of Sweet Dreams, who sang the UK's 1983 Eurovision entry, The Fizz are bubbling over with Eurovision history, experience and a lot of fun and laughter. Within minutes of meeting this fab four, it becomes apparent that Bobby M is as integral to the band as if he had always been part of it. That fact is underlined when they perform later in the evening. The Fizz are no trio plus one, but a quartet to be reckoned with once more.

We begin our interview by going back to when it all began for Bucks Fizz.

Cheryl: "We were built around Mike. The woman who put Bucks Fizz together, Nichola Martin, and Mike were friends. She wanted to do the demo of 'Making Your Mind Up' to put through as a possibility for Song For Europe. So, Mike did all the male vocals and Nichola did all the female vocals. When it got through, she had to put a group together. She asked Mike if he wanted to be in it and he said he wanted to be a solo singer."

Mike: "I didn't want to be in a band, but she said 'Don't worry about it. This song's not ever going to win. It's just something to put on your CV.' So I thought, okay, I'll do it then. And 36 years later…" [Mike laughs].

Do you have one particular memory which stands out from that time or were things so hectic that it is all just a blur?

Cheryl: "It was a blur but it was the most fantastic blur."
Jay: "I think it took us all by surprise."
Cheryl: "Not just surprise. It was a complete shock."
Jay: "It was a complete life change and meant a huge amount of travel around the world."
Mike: "We didn't even really realise we'd won Eurovision, it all happened so fast. We went everywhere… Australia, Japan, and the rest of Europe… we were in and out of there every day, weren't we?"
Cheryl: "Yes, and South Africa and Brazil. Our manager, she used to say 'Make sure you've got this in your diaries'… We all had Filofaxes in those days, which I really miss… she would say 'you've got to be in Austria on Monday, then you've got to come back 'cause you've got to do Top Of The Pops. Then the next day, you're flying off to Germany, and then you're coming back to routine the next single…"
Jay: "It was just very, very intense. We'd go on tour and then we'd have to fly back to do the vocals on the next album. We were recording the album for 22 hours a day, for ten days."

So, would you say you enjoy working more now? Are you more relaxed?

Mike: "No, it's not relaxed. It's boring now!"
Cheryl: "It's funny though, it's yes and no, because recording is a lot quicker because of the digital age, but because we've got

our new album [The F-Z of Pop, produced by Mike Stock and released September 2017] coming out we've got to do all this promotion. We won't get back tonight until three or four o'clock in the morning, then at nine o'clock we've got to get the train to go into London. All day we've got to do interviews. [Cheryl then reels off the band's schedule for the forthcoming week that is exhausting just to listen to] It's hectic again… and we're all a hundred and twenty three!"
Jay: "It's not like that 52 weeks a year, just 50!"

We move on to talking about The Fizz's current single 'Dancing In The Rain', which I heard being played recently on Radio 2. The band are keen to know whose show it was on. I tell them that it was likely to have been Ken Bruce, as that is when I usually listen to the station.

Cheryl: "Me too. I love Ken."
Mike: "I actually know him more as Bruce."
Cheryl: "We did an interview with him and Mike went 'Well, Bruce …'. I said, 'Mike, it's Ken Bruce!'
Mike: "He said 'Really, Nolan …' and I said 'My name's Mike, actually'. He said 'Yes, and I'm Ken!'. I saw him five years later and he went [Mike points to himself] 'Ken'. He's a great guy."

Ken Bruce is no stranger to Eurovision either, having begun commenting on the contest for Radio 2 in 1988. How do you think Eurovision today compares with that in the Eighties?

Cheryl: "It doesn't."
Jay: "Bigger."
Mike: "Yes, it is bigger but I preferred it in those days [Eighties]. It's all glamorised now, there are too many countries in it… and the voting… the countries vote, then the public vote and it all just falls apart, so there's no excitement to it."
Jay: "In our day, you heard the song once but now you can go on a whole promo tour, so it's not about hearing it once and it sticks with you, so you'll vote for it."
Cheryl: "I think, as a show though, it's better than ever before. It's bigger. They use fantastic pyrotechnics and wonderful special effects, so I think as a show it's better than ever. If you look back at when we won, the stage was small, it was done with an orchestra, it was all a bit… I don't know, a bit rumpty tumpty."

Mike: "No, but what about the sound? They're all miming."
Cheryl: "They're not miming!"
Mike: "So, where's the orchestra?"
Cheryl: "Well, there's a [backing] track but they're not miming. They're singing live. Sorry, we're just having a domestic!" [Cheryl laughs].

Is there anything you miss about the Eighties?

Mike: "You mean they're gone?"
Cheryl: "The hair, the clothes."
Bobby: "The mullets, the innocence…"
Cheryl: "Innocence? Did you say the innocence? You were innocent. You didn't drink, you didn't smoke."
Bobby: "Well, something had to change! To me, the Eighties always seemed clean and fun. Obviously I wasn't rock and rolling like them."
Mike: "We weren't rock and rolling. We had a clean-cut image, which I kept up, [adopts a mock serious pose] the other three didn't. They were terrible but I kept that image going. It's been hard work!"
Cheryl: "The Eighties were a lot of fun. It was a time of affluence."
Bobby: "Affluence?"
Cheryl: "As opposed to effluence! In the early part of the Eighties, there was more money around and people were enjoying themselves. The first five years of the Eighties were wonderful."
Jay: "Well, unless you happened to live in Brixton or somewhere else where there was a riot."
Bobby: "Yes, but you also had this new thing. You'd been through the glam rock of the Seventies, then Punk which all seemed dark and black to me, then suddenly the Eighties came along and it was more colourful… like these guys [Bobby indicates his fellow Fizz members]."
Jay: "We had Punk, which kind of took everything apart in the Seventies."
Cheryl: "It was very angry music, wasn't it?"
Bobby: "But after that, when you won Eurovision, the Durans came along, Wham!, people like that."
Mike: "Yes, and suddenly it was credible to like pop."
Jay: "There was room for everything… the independent record labels, they touted new talent so there was much more variety in music than we have now.

There was much more variety in the fashions of the decade too. You have worn some wonderful costumes over the years, but I have to ask specifically about what I consider to be the forerunner to Liz Hurley's 'safety pin' dress, the one Cheryl wore in 'The Land Of Make Believe' video.

Cheryl: "Oh yes, Jay found that. There was a little booth and a woman there who made all these leather outfits.
Jay: It was in the King's Road. It was a young designer, who was probably fresh out of one of the colleges. They would do all this leather stuff with studs, bright beads, chains…"
Mike: "Oh, I loved those chains!"
Jay: "It was unique, very different."

You didn't have a stylist then?

Cheryl: "No, no, no. Jay styled us. She used to make the outfits, like the 'Can't Stand The Heat' outfits, which were all made from chamois leather, dish cloths and things. She made them all."
Jay: "My parents were in showbiz, so when I was a kid my mum would always have a new dress on the sewing machine. At one point, I was making an outfit per day. It was my thing. In those days you didn't have mobile 'phones [to keep you busy] so I would make clothes. I started by making clothes for my dolls. It was my hobby to make clothes."
Cheryl: "She still makes them."
Jay: "You couldn't get what we wanted in the High Street. You'd have to go to Soho for things like sequins. You had to know the person just for them to let you see the good stuff. It was a very different world to today."
Cheryl: "She's made me a fantastic outfit for the next tour. She made it completely from scratch."

I look forward to seeing Jay's future creations. One last question before we say goodbye. What is your favourite Bucks Fizz song?

Jay: "I'm going to stick with 'Land Of Make Believe' because it was our biggest hit and I just think that visually, at that time, it appealed to both children and grandparents. It was an amazing track with a lot of visual attention. The video is great and it drove us to proper stardom."
Bobby: "'My Camera Never Lies' because it was the first time I ever met these guys. I did Song For Europe in 1982 and they were performing their new single, which happened to be 'My Camera Never Lies'. I just thought 'Wow!'.
Cheryl: "I would say 'Now Those Days Are Gone' because vocally I think it's brilliant. Not so much the lead vocal [performed by Mike], more the backing! [all laugh]
Mike: "My favourite song is 'You Love Love' [lead vocal by Cheryl]. My backing vocals are absolutely brilliant on it!

Eighties' Eurovision

Year	Winner	UK Entry
1980	What's Another Year by Johnny Logan (Ireland)	Love Enough For Two by Prima Donna
1981	Making Your Mind Up by Bucks Fizz	
1982	A Little Peace by Nicole (West Germany)	One Step Further by Bardo
1983	Si La Vie Est Cadeau by Corinne Hermès (Luxembourg)	I'm Never Giving Up by Sweet Dreams
1984	Diggi-Loo Diggi-Ley by Herrey's (Sweden)	Love Games by Belle & The Devotions
1985	La Det Swinge by Bobby Socks! (Norway)	Love Is by Vikki Watson
1986	J'aime La Vie by Sandra Kim (Belgium)	Runner In The Night by Ryder
1987	Hold Me Now by Johnny Logan (Ireland)	Only The Light by Rikki
1988	Ne Partez Pas Sans Moi by Celine Dion (Switzerland)	Go by Scott Fitzgerald
1989	Rock Me by Riva (Yugoslavia)	Why Do I Always Get It Wrong? by Live Report

GOING ONE STEP FURTHER WITH SALLY-ANN TRIPLETT

One of a handful of singers to enter the *Eurovision Song Contest* more than once, Sally-Ann Triplett first performed in the competition at the age of 18, as part of the group Prima Donna. The six-piece UK entry, which also featured Lance Aston (brother of Bucks Fizz's Jay) and sisters Kate and Jane Robbins, came third in 1980 with the song 'Love Enough For Two'. Two years later, Sally-Ann partnered Stephen Fischer in the duo Bardo, to represent the UK for a second time. Despite only reaching seventh place in the contest, their entry 'One Step Further' went on to become a No. 2 hit in the UK singles chart.

What first attracted you to the Eurovision Song Contest?

"I didn't really get attracted to it. It wasn't like I sat at home and thought 'Ooh, I must be in the Eurovision," she replies. "The first time, I was actually at college and my singing teacher, Mary Hammond, put me up for a session." A renowned vocal coach, Mary includes Chris Martin, Guy Garvey and Florence Welch amongst the artists she has taught. "I did this session and out of that I got an audition, then I did the audition and I got Prima Donna. It's so long ago now that it's really hard to remember." Her second foray into the contest came about when "I was doing pantomime in Cambridge and Steve [Fischer] was in panto with me. We became boyfriend and girlfriend, and he had actually been asked to be with Bucks Fizz the year before but he couldn't do it because he was committed to something else.

After we finished the panto, we were going out on our first day back in London. He said 'I've just got to pop in and sing for someone because I might be doing Eurovision', so I went with him, just as his girlfriend. I was sat in Mayfair Studios in Primrose

> **" Also, because Bucks Fizz had won the year before and, basically, the BBC didn't want to host it again. We were the bookies' favourite by a mile.**

Hill and Nichola Martin came out and saw me sitting there." Nichola Martin and her then husband Andy Hill were responsible for creating Bucks Fizz. Nichola went on to manage the band while Andy continued to write the band's hit singles, including 'My Camera Never Lies', 'Land of Make Believe' and 'If You Can't Stand The Heat'. The pair also entered the Song For Europe contest in 1981 with 'Have You Ever Been In Love?' as part of the group Paris. Although they had little success with the track, when it was covered a year later by Leo Sayer, he took it to No. 10 in the UK charts.

Sally-Ann continues "She took a look at me and said 'I know you', obviously from two years before, and asked me to come in and sing with Steve. Because we had been singing together [in panto] we were kind of like soul mates. We could feel when each other was breathing. We just sang really well together, we had

that connection. We sang the song together, and there and then she [Nichola] said 'Yep, I want you two to represent us. I want you to be in my Song For Europe.' So, we went from doing panto, then meeting on our first day off, to forming a band for Song For Europe, and representing Britain a few months later. When I look back on it, it was really incredible. It was a great time, but it found me, and I didn't find it."

When Bardo competed in the Eurovision Song Contest on 24th April 1982, the UK had been at war with Argentina for three weeks, fighting over the sovereignty of the Falkland Islands. Germany's entrant Nicole took to the stage in Harrogate, Yorkshire looking like she had wandered off a Sixties' hippy protest march. As she strummed her acoustic guitar and sang about 'A Little Peace', there was little doubt as to who would be that year's winner.

"All of that stuff was against us," admits Sally-Ann. "Also, because Bucks Fizz had won the year before and, basically, the BBC didn't want to host it again. We were the bookies' favourite by a mile. It was a great song, which was written by Simon Jefferis, who became a good friend of ours. It was produced by Andy [Hill], who did all of Bucks Fizz's songs, and it was a good track. That year, we were so the best song!"

Who chose the outfit you wore for the Eurovision Song Contest?

"The white dress and little white knickers?" laughs Sally-Ann. "My white knickers were from Williams, which was a sports shop in Finchley. But it was Nichola [who chose the outfit]. That was made for me, that little white dress. I still have that dress; my mum has it.

Dollar were out at the time, and not quite boy/girl next door. They were similar to us but we were more innocent than them. It was weird because they [Bardo's record company] gave us what to wear and they gave us the song, and a few months down the line we went in to see our record label, CBS Epic, and they said 'Well, what's your image?' but they'd been giving us our image. It was a bit of a shock to think now what do we do? We did two more singles after that, and I had like rags in my hair, and I don't know what was going on really. But it was fun. It was really, really good fun.

I was young. I was twenty, and when I think back on it now, it seems kind of ridiculous. It doesn't happen anymore really, unless you're a really big name, but back then they really looked after you. They would pick me up in a white stretch limo outside my mum and dad's house, and the neighbours would be like 'Ooh look, there's Sally-Ann going off." A brilliant, brilliant time. I can't think of anything bad to say about it."

Why do you think we did love Eurovision so much during the Eighties?

"I think there was an innocence with it all. Yes, it was political back then and it was political the year that I did it, the second time, but now it's crazy, bonkers. You literally know who's going to vote for who. That innocent, fun factor has left it. When we [the UK] first started out, we put forward our good people. We put forward Cliff and Lulu, amazing people to represent British music. We don't do that ever... it's just a joke now."

So, you wouldn't be tempted to enter the competition again?
"Nah," she laughs.

What about your son? [Sally-Ann's son Max Milner appeared in the first series of The Voice UK]

"No, oh my god no, never. Not in a million years. He's very, very passionate about his music. That's the thing though, isn't it? If you're a passionate musician and if you love what you do and you write your own stuff, Eurovision is a joke. It wasn't though. It was sort of in a different light and everyone was quite patriotic back then. It was just a different time and a different world when I did it."

Since then, you've had some wonderful stage roles. Do you have a favourite musical?

"I think my favourite one that I've done in the West End is 'Anything Goes'. It started at the National and then we went to Drury Lane for a year. Being in an actual musical like that was incredible. I've been lucky enough to do so many fantastic roles. I loved playing Rizzo in 'Grease', I loved doing 'Chicago', I loved being in 'Acorn Antiques'. There are loads."
Sally-Ann also got to star alongside Jimmy Nail in The Last Ship.
"That was on Broadway. He was wonderful. He's a good friend of mine, we keep in touch. He's amazing. There's literally nothing that man hasn't done. He'd sit there and he'd talk to you about when he was done for grievous bodily harm and how long he was inside for," she says. "Then we'd go and sing a song together. He was wonderful though and, of course, he left the show and then I got some bloke called Sting. I mean, you know, he wasn't a patch on Jimmy Nail," jokes Sally-Ann. "It was very hard. I had to kiss him every night. It was awful," she laughs.

Would you say musical theatre is your true passion then?

"No, it's such a weird thing. I don't really know how to explain it other than when I was little, the thing that I really wanted to do was to perform. I knew I wanted to perform and I knew I was a bit of a show-off, but apart from being a show-off, it was a thing that really made me happy and I'm still like that. I don't sit at home listening to musical theatre, and it's not like I feel I need to be in musicals. I just wanted to be in the business. I think one of my favourite things that I've done was when I was in a band. After we did Bardo, I was in a band called Co-op City. We were on The Tube, we were managed by the Eurythmics' manager, did loads of gigs in London.

I've done lots of different things. I was a backing vocalist at one point in my life. I did backing vocals for Sam Brown, and sessions for Sam Fox. She had an album that came out and before she did that album, the record company offered me that song [Sally-Ann sings 'Touch Me (I Want Your Body)'].

I was like ... no-oo, I don't think that's really me. But I ended up recording all the album for her to copy. So, I recorded all the tracks and then she had someone to kind of listen to and do the album."

What a fantastic story. I expect many people will be surprised to learn you were a voice guide for Samantha Fox.

"I've got lots of funny stories like that. I remember singing in Simon Jefferis' flat one night and there was a 'phone call. Someone said 'Are you free to come and sing?' It was 11 o'clock at night and I said 'Yeah, alright. If you send a cab for me, I'll get there. I got to this studio and it was for Limahl. It was back in the

> ## We just sang really well together, we had that connection.

day when you had to re-record your tracks for Top of The Pops. So, I went in and I recorded 'Never Ending Story' for Top of The Pops. Then I saw this girl who had been miming to my voice. I saw her come out of the Tube one day and I went up to her and said 'Hey, were you on Top of The Pops with Limahl?' and she was all very like 'yeah, yeah that was me'. I said 'Oh right, that was my voice you were miming to!' It was funny."

Is there anything you miss about the Eighties?

"Everything, just everything! When you look back now, as you get further and further and further away, the music just seems ridiculous, it's so good. I love what I used to wear in the Eighties. I kind of felt that you could sort of go for anything, really, and I was a lot younger so I would. I'd go to Camden and buy this long jumper that had these green stripes going down. I thought I looked marvellous in it. It was really awful, looking back!"

IN CONVERSATION WITH
MR. EUROVISION

The only performer to have twice won the Eurovision Song Contest, Johnny Logan first came to the public's attention in 1980 when, representing Ireland, he sung the winning entry *'What's Another Year'*. Seven years later he repeated his achievement, this time with his own composition *'Hold Me Now'*. To top off his own personal success, the Australian-born singer and songwriter then went on to pen the 1992 winning entry *'Why Me*?', sung by Ireland's Linda Martin.

What felt better, winning the Eurovision the first time in 1980, winning it with your own song in 1987 or writing the winning entry in 1992?

"I suppose it's like having three children, you know. They were all different. I'd have to say winning with my own song, with 'Hold Me Now' was the most complete, but 1980 was such a surprise. When I went to The Hague, I was the third favourite. The bookies all used to turn up as well as the record companies and the media people, and when I turned up 'What's Another Year' was the third favourite to win. Then the day I turned up, I think they took one look at me and I dropped out of the Top Ten!

All I thought about with the first song in 1980 was making the people back home proud, not letting down the country. I never thought about winning. When I won, it was such a shock. Really, it took me and everybody around me by surprise."
When he entered again in 1987, Johnny had placed the bar in the highest position possible.

"When you win one time, there's only one place you can come if you do it again. So, anything except first place would have been a failure really. There was so much riding on it, the rebuilding of my career and everything. The stress involved with it alone... I think, if I remember rightly, they had to take in the costume that I wore three times, because I lost so much weight. I couldn't eat all week. That suit is actually now in the Abba Museum in Stockholm. It's been there for the last year. It's in a glass case, I think. There are those who think I should be in a museum somewhere," he jokes.

What was the impact of winning the Eurovision Song Contest on your career?

"The Eurovision Song Contest, although it's been very good to me and I'm very grateful and proud of the songs I won with, it really was, for me, about representing your country back then. It was a means to an end in so much as in Ireland, if you were a solo singer, it was very, very hard to work outside of Ireland. Bands got to go over and play, and record companies came to see them, but there wasn't that kind of avenue for solo singers. Eurovision, if you won it back in the Eighties, it was a huge thing. I won it on a Saturday, I think it was, they pressed the records on Sunday and they started to chart on Monday. That whole side of the business is gone now. When I look back at it, I enjoyed Eurovision the same way everybody else did at that time, but I never saw it as being the huge thing in my life it turned out to be."

Was getting a foot in the door of the music industry what attracted you to Eurovision then?

"It was the only way really to build a career outside of Ireland. I suppose, like everyone else who's in the music industry, you want to build an international career. My father was an Irish tenor who travelled the world singing, and that's what I wanted. I wanted a lifetime in music, travelling all over the world singing, and that's what I ended up with."

Was your father a major influence in your decision to go into music?

"This is going to sound very strange, I'm sure, but not really. My father had rheumatoid arthritis. He was a lovely singer and a really lovely man but he was a very insecure man because he couldn't work with his hands. To live as a singer, it's not a very safe life. It's a very insecure life, and I think that insecurity was not something he wanted for any of his children. We were always made aware of that but I had no choice. I tried to be an electrician. I tried everything. I was awful. I was a shit electrician," he laughs. "Terrible. I really was awful. I look back on it and think, I wonder whatever happened to those buildings I wired. Are they still standing? I used to go into work with a guitar and a tool case, and at lunchtime I would play guitar for the other guys that I worked with, the fitters and welders. Music was just there for me. Music was the backdrop to my life."

" I'm very grateful and proud of the songs I won with.

That musical backdrop is reflected in the variety of styles on your album 'It Is What It Is', which was released earlier this year. Who have been your musical influences?

"Sometimes I think I've been around since God was a boy, so my influences go way, way back. I started off with Led Zeppelin, Black Sabbath, and then I got into Cat Stevens and Neil Young. Then I went through my soul phase... Marvin Gaye and all of those... then it was all the bands from the late Seventies like Little Feat and Earth, Wind & Fire. I love music, any kind of music as long as it's played well. I really loved Thin Lizzy but I realised fairly early that my kind of thing was really singer/songwriter."

So, is the album a melting pot of all of those?

"I think what this is... over the years, you know, you grew up in Ireland in the late Seventies and Eighties, and when you were in bands you had to do every style of music. You couldn't make a living from just playing one [style]. I played in traditional Irish bars, in showband dance halls, in bands in pubs, and you learn to play everything really. I suppose that was one of the faults of my career, that when I did win Eurovision in 1980, I remember somebody from a record company saying "Well, what do you want to sing now?" and I was like I don't really know. I'd love to be the lead singer with Duran Duran or something like this, but apart from looking like him, I couldn't be him. So, I had this real tug between me and the record company because they wanted like a singing version of Bobby Crush, who was a piano player who mums loved, and I wanted to go the other way. I was into The Clash and what was happening in the charts then. There was always this pull between me and record companies... what I wanted to do and what they wanted me to record. I lived most of the Eighties and most of my life, from a recording point of view, with compromise. Looking back, it wasn't a particularly good thing, but it was the only way forward at that particular point in my life.

When I did this album, I funded it myself and released through Universal. They distribute it but I have my own record label [Shake It Easy] and it will not be streamed. I'm one of these people who don't agree with streaming. I do think that it's part of the music industry and will be part of the music industry for all the years to come but at the moment, the way they break down the profits from streaming the artist gets nothing basically. It's unbelievable."

Would you consider entering Eurovision again, either as a contestant or songwriter?

"To be honest, I haven't really thought about white Zimmer frames or white wheelchairs," he laughs. "I think sometimes it's a bit like being a champion boxer, there's always a fight or a song in you but for me to do Eurovision again, I'd have to give up so much of my life to be involved with another artist, because it wouldn't be enough to write the song. I'd have to work with the artist on how to present it and how to sing it, and I think that would just take too much [time]. I don't have that much time left. I'm so busy with my own stuff, with what I'm doing. I've also recorded the music this year for the Leipzig Symphony Orchestra for an Irish classical album which will be out next year sometime.

There's talk of a movie being made about me, between 1980 and '87, and my life. There was a documentary done on me which was shown in Ireland around Christmas, and looks like it's going to be shown all over Europe. There's so much happening around me, in general, I don't know where I would find the time. I'm actually busier now than I ever was. 'Hold Me Now' will be the music for the new Smart car ad that's going out all over the world, and my diary is full until 2019 touring."

Why do you think Eurovision is not as much fun as it used to be?

"For me, I think where the Eurovision is now is it's reflective of where the music industry is now. I mean, if you look at X Factor and Popstars... that is the bar level people look at as being successful in the music industry. You get the odd ones that break through from America, the big ones, or you get the really good artists like Adele or Ed Sheeran, who cut through from another background, but they're very, very few and far between.
The thing is the people who do those shows, they don't call them singers when they win, they call them stars. They have that name immediately. That was a word that you had to earn, and not just one or two records. It tool years and years in the industry before you earned the right to call yourself a star, when I was growing up. That doesn't exist anymore. I think that the music industry and Eurovision in particular represent that now. It's just a Eurovision version of the same show."

In 1985, Johnny was one of the artists who performed on The Crowd's "You'll Never Walk Alone", a track recorded to raise funds for those affected by the Bradford City fire disaster.

How did you come to be part of The Crowd in 1985?

"In the Eighties, I was signed to Sony Records and I think when they were looking for artists, I was one of the artists who were around," he says modestly of his involvement in the project. "They called and asked if I would sing on the song. I turned up and met Gerry [Marsden] and all the other people doing it... Paul McCartney's band, Lemmy, lots of different people. There were some Irish artists there as well. It was a great vibe at that, a really, really great vibe. Meeting people like Francis Rossi and some of the guys from Status Quo. To be honest, and you probably hear this all the time, it was really fun in the Eighties, the music business in general. There was a lot more fun than there is now. I look back and say 'yes, maybe I could have behaved myself a bit better' but at least I didn't live on mineral water and Farley's rusks!"

Is there anything you miss about the Eighties?

"Everything," he chuckles. "My hair, the colour of my hair. These days it's blond, natural blond. It said it on the bottle! I'm lucky I kept my hair but I look back on it, and I see this little boy from the Eighties and I look at myself now... it is what it is. That's where the title of the album came from."
I comment that it is easier for men as they look more distinguished as they age, whereas women just tend to look old.

"I would disagree with that," replies Johnny. "Those days are gone, I think. There's a lot of cougars around, thank God. Some of them without good eyesight and some who haven't been to Specsavers!"

80'S EUROVISION WORDSEARCH

```
N O S R B B U S K C O S Y B B O B I K S
S T S K E T U J O H N N Y L O G N B I Y
T N C U Z D J C O T A K I O B L A R K E
C M O F Z I Y K K I S N M O B R E Y K R
E A T I I O N R U S W E N M D M R D I R
L E T L T J H N N E F E T O M A E R D E
I R F I G O O A I M I I N D D R O C S H
N D I V U H V I C R T B Z K R A D E M S
E E T E T I K E O E Z D C Z E M M L A B
N G Z R R K B K D H G O E R A L D I E O
O Z G E O Z F O I E S R B J U T U N R B
S Z E P F Z M U B N H A A O H R V E D P
T U R I K K I N G N U T R H E O I D T R
A B A B B U K R B I B O D N R P N I E I
W I L D E R A I A R I Y N N M E I O E M
I F D J E Y R V R O V A J Y A R C N W A
K N H O W E D Y D C R E O L L E O G S S
K I M S A D N R T W N N H O C V L A L D
I O N N S R A Z I A O N N G O I E L B O
V S T A W Y S Z N T S I N A R L D O E N
P R I M A B U C G K S F I N Z Z B A R B
```

Bardo	Belle And The Devotions	Bobbysocks
Bucks Fizz	Celine Dion	Corinne Hermes
Herrey's	Johnny Logan	Live Report
Nicole	Prima Donna	Rikki
Riva	Ryder	Sandra Kim
Scott Fitzgerald	Sweet Dreams	Vikki Watson

Answers at back of book

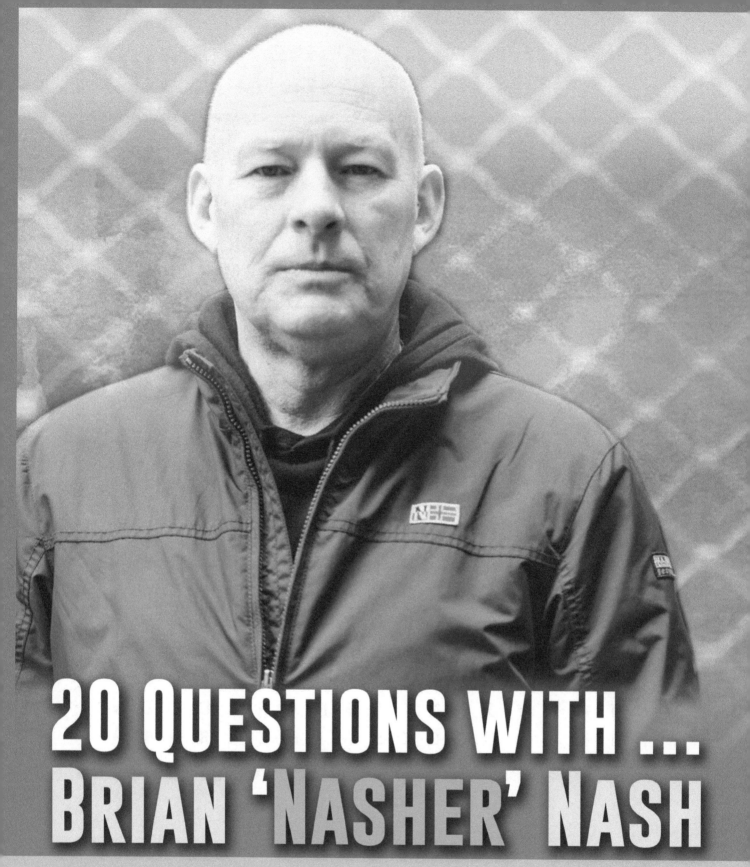

20 QUESTIONS WITH ...
BRIAN 'NASHER' NASH

When their debut single 'Relax' reached number one in January 1984, Frankie Goes To Hollywood embarked on a year that would see them dominating both the airwaves and our TV screens. The band's next two singles 'Two Tribes' and 'The Power of Love' also reached the top spot that year, seeing them equal a record held by fellow Scousers Gerry & The Pacemakers for their first three singles topping the charts. Their subsequent releases saw the band spend a total of 102 weeks in the UK Top 40, fifty of those in the Top 10.

Former Frankie Goes To Hollywood guitarist Brian Nash continues to write, perform and record, with his latest album '432-1 Open The Vein', having been released on his own Babylon Pink label. Here Nasher reveals his answers to our 80s-style questions.

1 What is your favourite 80's TV programme?
Porridge. I was chuffed to meet John Dair (Harry Grout's sidekick "Crusher") when he appeared in a couple of Frankie videos. He was the half naked fat guy in the 'Relax' video. Lovely man, sadly no longer with us.

2 What was your worst fashion mistake of the 80s?
Leather chaps. Thankfully, I wore jeans underneath. I would like several other offences to be taken into account.

3 What was your favourite subject at school?
Geography and English, largely because of the two teachers who taught it at my secondary school: Mr Finn and Mr Towey.

4 What job would you have done if you hadn't been a musician?
I would have continued being an electrician probably.

5 Who was your teenage crush?
Kate Bush or Pauline Murray.

6 What was your first car?
I shared a Ford Fiesta 1.4s with my wife but a few years later I had my own Ford Fiesta XR2.

7 What do you miss most about the Eighties?
THE HAIR!!!

8 What was the first single you ever bought?
'Poppa Joe' by The Sweet.

9 Where did you perform your first gig?
St Teresa's school canteen in Liverpool, with a band called Smuzz who played punk covers.

10 Which five people, living or dead, would be your ideal dinner guests?
My Mum and Dad, Bill Hicks, George Carlin and Jesus. I have some questions for him.

11 Who would play you in your biopic?
Sean Bean.

12 Which pet hate would you consign to Room 101?
People who don't acknowledge your gesture when you give way whilst driving.

13 What makes you angry?
Intolerance, inequality, greed and Tories.

14 What is the last book you read?
Fiction: The Ragged Trousered Philanthropists and Non Fiction: Half A Million Women.

15 What are you most proud of?
My wife and children and my impressive collection of aftershave.

16 What would be your perfect day?
Breakfast with my wife in Gijon, an afternoon of playing Mahjong with my mates, and a Talk Talk reunion gig in the evening with anyone who wanted to come with me.

17 What is the best Christmas present you've ever had?
A white Grant Les Paul copy guitar in 1979. That's when the trouble started.

18 And the worst?
A bottle of Brut 33 that myself and my mates recycled every year. It disappeared in the mid Nineties. It was so old, Henry Cooper had a full head of hair and Kevin Keegan was still at Liverpool.

19 What do you want for Christmas this year?
The disarming and destruction of all weapons, nuclear and non-nuclear. Or some socks and Maynard's Wine Gums.

20 What are your hopes for the future?
To see hope and unity defeat despair and division after extra time and penalties.

Growing Up With Jamie Days

Thursday 7th March 1985
The Madonna video was on Top of the Pops. It's really good. It's at No.5. Dad said she's taking off Marilyn Monroe, whatever that is.

Friday 29th March
Those stickers are from a magazine called Smash Hits. There are free ones with it this week so I bought it. It's brilliant, it's got words to all the songs in it including things like Supergran and others. Next week there's a brilliant poster of Madonna in it in bed. I was showing everybody. My issue is all ripped though cos I rolled it up and used it to beat up Carl. Day quite okay really.

Friday 12th April
Me and Katie went to get the new Smash Hits from the paper shop. Mum says I can have it every week now. It's got a massive Madonna poster in it. I put it up in the playroom. We went to see Auntie Connie and showed it to her. She thought Smash Hits was Madonna's surname! Me and Katie cracked up. Nik Kershaw's record company tried to hide his wife. We think that's awful. There was an ace new TV show on tonight called C.A.T.S. Eyes. It was great.

Saturday 4th May
Had to go get new school trousers this morning. Started reading 'Forever'. Haven't got to any rude bits yet.

Sunday 5th May
Woke up at 10:00 and read more of 'Forever'. I love Jamie. She's dead cool. She said "hate and war are bad words but fuck isn't" which is just so true. Listened to 'Move Closer'. It's dead sexy. I only wear a t-shirt to bed now and nothing else. Went to see Nana and then played out this afternoon. Roller boots are making a comeback. Saw 'That's Life'.

Saturday 11 May
Went to Charlotte, Melanie and Rebecca's tonight. We had a right laugh. Looked in her old Smash Hits for a penfriend for me but we couldn't find one. She has an ace poster of Madonna sat on a wooden washing machine type thing wearing an orange jumper. I want it. There was a fire at the football in Bradford. It was really bad. Ray and Dad were watching it all night. Mum thinks the Dennis's might have been there.

Wednesday 5th June
Boring day at school. Angela hasn't finished 'Forever' yet. I need it back now. Alistair reckons his middle names are Ralph and Stanley! He banged his fist on the table when he heard Michael calls his knob Ralph. Martin fancies Carol. Got Smash Hits with the free Madonna postcard.

Tuesday 11th June
Fenton brought 'Forever' back. They have both read it now. I read it again … well, just the rude parts. Asked Sean what it means when you come. He says it's the best part of sex apparently. He hasn't heard of 'Forever'. We are doing the lifecycle of the frog in Science. Won't be long until we do humans now! I drew a sperm. There's a strike tomorrow.

Growing Up With Jamie Days

Saturday 13th July

It was the gala today. We went down after the start of Live Aid. It was a bit rubbish. There was a thing where you sit on a pole and try and hit each other off with pillows. Mazz went on but she was knocked off. I didn't go on it. The bouncy castle was good. Went on that 3 times. After tea we went down to the field to search for money. I found 75p. Mazz found £1. We played out on our roller skates after that until Madonna was on Live Aid. She didn't sing anything I had heard of before. Sean said he might have recognised one of the songs. Dad said he thought she was good. Went to bed at 1am. Sean stayed up to the end.

Sunday 21st July

Spent ages waiting to hear 'Into The Groove' on the radio so I could tape it. Finally managed to get it. It's really good, it doesn't sound anything like when she sang it at Live Aid.

Saturday 27th July

Charlotte, Melanie, Rebecca and their mum and dad came today. We had a barbecue and played 'Into the Groove' over and over until Mum told us to stop it. They said I've got the words wrong and that it's "at night I lock the door where no one else can see" and not "at night like to go where no one else can see". I wore my t-shirt that says David Essex and they laughed at it. Apparently, he's a pop star from the 70s. I only wear it because I like the colour.

Wednesday 31st July

Went down to the village with Katie. We got the new Smash Hits. It's got the words to 'Into The Groove' and Charlotte was right about them, which makes me mad. There's also a Madonna Personal File. Her favourite saying is "Where's the beef?". Her film is out on 6th September but it's a 15 so I might not be able to see it. She's in Penthouse as well and I definitely won't get to see that, but I don't know if I want to.

Sunday 11th August

Mum, Dad and Sean went to cricket today and I was allowed to stay at home. Katie came round, we listened to 'Like a Virgin'. We both like 'Angel' because Madonna has a dirty laugh at the beginning and Katie does an impression of Marky going "in de skies". We made up a song about Auntie Pam called 'Like A Galleon' to the tune of 'Like A Virgin'. It's dead funny. It's about how fat she is.

Saturday 17th August

It was on the news today that Madonna got married. I was up in the fields and Dad shouted me down to come and watch it. He said to me "your luck's out, son". She got married on a cliff top but you couldn't really see any of it properly. Emma came back from Spain. Her nose is peeling.

Tuesday 3rd September

Back to school tomorrow. I am looking forward to seeing Alistair and all that lot. Heard the new chart. All Madonna's singles are going down. Mum's read 'Are You There God? It's Me, Margaret' and then wanted to talk to me about periods! For God's sake. I refused. I am not having sex talk with her!

Tuesday 17th September

The new chart was out today. Madonna is the highest new entry at No.10 with 'Angel'. It might get to No.1. Dad let me stay up to watch Film 85 because Desperately Seeking Susan was on it. It looks so good. Dad said he might let me go see it. It got a good review.

Saturday 26th October

Today was unbelievable. At last I got to see Desperately Seeking Susan. Mazz asked her dad and he agreed to take us. It was a dream come true, although we almost didn't get in. Mazz had put loads of make-up on, to try and look older, and I went first. They didn't ask how old I was, then Katie went and she got in okay, but they asked Mazz and she went "f-f-f-f-f-fourteen".

I thought they were going to turn us away but, thank God, they didn't. It was absolutely brilliant. Madonna is brilliant in it. The best bits are where they dance to 'Into the Groove' in a nightclub and at the end, when Madonna is kidnapped by the grease ball. I want to see it again. Katie and Mazz loved it too. I love Madonna so much.

Follow Jamie on Twitter: @1980sDiaries
Jamie Days' 1984 and 1985 Diaries are available on Amazon, and 1986 is coming soon!

FAVOURITE FIVE

Regular listeners to the My 80s radio show will be familiar with the Favourite Five feature, in which guests choose and discuss their five favourite songs from the Eighties. Here are some of the guests who have appeared on the show, along with their choices.

David Ball – Soft Cell

1 Love Action by The Human League

2 Burning Car by John Foxx

3 Fade To Grey by Visage

4 (We Don't Need This) Fascist Groove Thang by Heaven 17: "I think the title is quite relevant really for a lot of the horrible political, quasi religious stuff that's going on at the moment. It's also because I was always very much into the early Human League, with Ian Craig Marsh and Martyn Ware [who went on to form Heaven 17 with Glenn Gregory]. I love the sound and the sentiment of this track."

5 Duel by Propaganda

Brian Nash – Frankie Goes To Hollywood

1 The Downtown Lights by The Blue Nile: "I've been a massive fan of The Blue Nile ever since I heard 'Hats' [the album which features 'The DownTown Lights']. It's just stunning and Paul Buchanan, I just love his voice. I think he's probably my favourite singer of all time."

2 Life's What You Make It by Talk Talk

3 Shipbuilding by Elvis Costello

4 Rush Hour by Jane Wiedlin

5 Blue Monday by New Order

Dennis Seaton

Dennis Seaton – Musical Youth

1 Don't Turn Around by Aswad

2 Roses Are Red by The Mac Band: "The song kind of embodied new jack swing. Roses are red, violets are blue... such simple two lines but they turned it into something fantastic. You can't help but move because the beat is the jack swing of the time."

3 Come On Eileen by Dexys Midnight Runners

4 Mirror In The Bathroom by The Beat

5 Many Rivers To Cross by UB40

Nick van Eede

Nick van Eede – Cutting Crew

1 Pale Shelter by Tears for Fears

2 The Whole of the Moon by The Waterboys

3 Carnation by The Jam

4 Need You Tonight by INXS

5 I Still Haven't Found What I'm Looking For by U2: "This song means a lot to me from some of the darker times in my life, in my career. After you've had a big hit, and then you have your three or four years out there being pop stars, unless you are U2, it normally comes to an end fairly quickly. I used to lock myself up in my studio every night for about two years, and this was the song I put on to test the sound. It's one of the greatest sounding records ever made, I think, but it would be my inspiration for finding what that is. Of course, I still haven't found what I'm looking for... a beautiful irony!"

Peter Coyle – The Lotus Eaters

1 The Sensual World by Kate Bush

2 Biko by Peter Gabriel

3 Ashes To Ashes by David Bowie

4 Sign O' The Times by Prince: "The lyric is just beyond belief... the depth. The genius of Prince was he had so much talent and he just does it... just locks in. Once that music energy is in him, there's no stopping him. That man was an absolute genius, and that whole album just captured everything that was brilliant about Prince. He was at his peak then for me."

5 Girl On A Swing by Andy Summers & Robert Fripp

Peter Coyle

Clark Datchler – Johnny Hates Jazz

1. Forbidden Colours by David Sylvian and Ryuichi Sakamoto

2. Life's What You Make It by Talk Talk: "It's indicative of the time, I think. One of the powerful things about the Eighties is those involved in music had grown up with a strong songwriting ethos, which merged with technology. Some of the best music came out of that decade, and Talk Talk were one of the best bands of their time. They were never celebrity orientated, they were slightly left-field, but the songs have stood the test of time. What a great message as well... life's what you make it."

3. Sowing The Seeds Of Love by Tears For Fears

4. Don't Dream It's Over by Crowded House

5. Silent Running by Mike & The Mechanics

Ian Donaldson – H2O

1. Slave To Love by Bryan Ferry

2. Quiet Life by Japan

3. Drive by The Cars

4. Absolute Beginners by David Bowie

5. Heaven by Psychedelic Furs: "'Heaven' is just a beauty. Richard Butler does something with his voice.. it's got a slight kinda husk to it. I think he's tapped into a different area of love with 'Heaven'. It's not all flowers and candy. He gives it this sweet backing but there's also something quite dark about it at the same time. There is light at the end of the tunnel, and half the time it's an oncoming train, but this time maybe it is just going to be sunshine."

Andy Kyriacou – Modern Romance

1. The Reflex by Duran Duran

2. Easy Lover by Philip Bailey with Phil Collins

3. Sexual Healing by Marvin Gaye

4. Let's Dance by David Bowie

5. Walk This Way by Aerosmith: "I remember I did this drumathon [for Children In Need] and I drummed for 15 hours non-stop. There was this DJ playing songs in parallel, and he played all these upbeat songs to play along to.. didn't give me a break. When this song came on, there was the biggest smile on my face because it's such a good beat, with the rap element and the rock element. Coming on at that point, it kind of lifted me because I'd been drumming for hours and hours."

Clark Datchler

Junior Giscombe

Photo credit: cjansenphotography.com

Junior Giscombe

(Note: Some of Junior's choices were not released in the Eighties, but if you listen to his interview you will learn why they were allowed)

1. I'm In Love by Evelyn King

2. Never Too Much by Luther Vandross

3. Let Your Feeling Show by Earth, Wind & Fire

4. Don't Let It Go To Your Head by Jean Carn

5. Ribbon In The Sky by Stevie Wonder: "I lost one of my daughters [Jenique lost her battle with MS in May 2017] and this was her favourite song. She used to come out and sing with me and to warm her up, this would be the song that she would sing. I know that those family members who will be listening in will smile when they hear this song. It's such a beautiful song.

David Brewis — The Kane Gang

1. Videotheque by Dollar: "It struck me when I first heard it way back then, and still does now, it has the most amazing production. Trevor Horn could take the most disco-y, pop act and just produce such a brilliant song. The sound is huge... like a hundred miles high. It's very tongue-in-cheek and quite camp, but I still think it's a very powerful record."

2. I'm In Love With A German Film Star by The Passions

3. It's A Love Thing by The Whispers

4. All Night Long by Mary Jane Girls

5. Friends by Shalamar

To hear the Favourite Five interviews in full, plus the chosen tracks, visit my Mixcloud page: Sarah Lewis #My80s, where all past My 80s radio shows are archived.

SOLUTIONS AND ACKNOWLEDGEMENTS

80'S SWEETS AND TREATS

80'S SPORT

80'S EUROVISION

88

LYRICALLY CHALLENGED:

1. Propaganda - Duel 2. Shakin' Stevens - Oh Julie 3. Luther Vandross - Never Too Much 4. AC/DC - Back In Black 5. The Lotus Eaters - The First Picture of You 6. Ultravox - Love's Great Adventure 7. The Rah Band - Clouds Across The Moon 8. The Bangles - Walk Like An Egyptian 9. Pet Shop Boys - Rent 10. Peter Gabriel - Sledgehammer 11. The Cure - The Caterpillar 12. Baltimora - Tarzan Boy 13. Imagination - Body Talk 14. Bad Manners - Lorraine 15. Dr Hook - Sexy Eyes 16. The Mobiles - Drowning In Berlin 17. Rick Astley - She Wants To Dance With Me 18. Gary Moore and Phil Lynott - Out In The Fields 19. Howard Jones - Pearl In The Shell 20. Strawberry Switchblade - Since Yesterday

QUIZZING TIMES:

1. 12 (7 + 5) 2. 32 (1999 - 1967) 3. 25 (17 +8) 4. 1 (69 - 68) 5. 1814 (1814 + 0) 6. 6 (2 x3) 7. 5 (500 ÷ 100) 8. 21 (3 x 7) 9. 4 (16 ÷ 4) 10. 8 (2 x 4)

80'S TV & FILM CROSSWORD

Across:
1. Just Good Friends 8. Moonlighting 9. CE (Clint Eastwood) 10. Roger 11. DN (De Niro) 12. PY (Paula Yates) 13. Ape 15. AC (Andy Crane) 17. Fools 18. Alan 19. Lost 21. Sid 22. Nicholas 25. And 27. LD (Les Dennis) 28. Superstore 33. Colour 34. Dex Dexter 36. St. 38. ES (Elisabeth Shue) 39. Tom 42. Laugh 43. Emu 44. Century

Down:
1. Joe 2. Two 3. Only 4. Fagin 5. Emily 6. Dogs 7. Knight Rider 8. Meg 9. Cocoon 11. Del 12. PC 14. Paul 15. Any 16. Blind 20. Odd 21. Sale Of The 23. One 24. Saturday 26. Bradley 28. Six 29. Pte 30. Rats 31. RC (Reg Cox) 32. Horses 35. Date 36. SG (Steve Guttenberg) 37. Out 40. On 41. MT (Montana) 42. LR (Linda Robson)

POP QUIZ

1. The Jets 2. Howard Jones 3. Manhattan Skyline 4. Richard Skinner 5. Some Guys Have All The Luck 6. Break Dance Party 7. Alabama Song 8. Elton John 9. Madonna 10. The Specials 11. Rain or Shine (number 2 in 1986) 12. 4: Wake Me Up Before You Go-Go, Freedom, I'm Your Man and Edge of Heaven 13. Big Audio Dynamite 14. Cherelle 15. 7 (3 solo, 4 with Genesis) 16. Whistle Down The Wind 17. Tennessee 18. I Want That Man 19. Heaven Knows I'm Miserable Now 20. Simultaneous number 1 single and album 21. Coventry 22. Beverly Hills Cop 23. Squeeze 24. OMD (Orchestral Manoeuvres In The Dark) 25. The Bed's Too Big Without You 26. You Spin Me Round (Like A Record) by Dead Or Alive 27. Levi's 501 jeans 28. 9: I Just Can't Stop Loving You, Bad, The Way You Make Me Feel, Man In The Mirror, Dirty Diana, Another Part of Me, Smooth Criminal, Leave Me Alone (on CD version only) and Liberian Girl 29. Modern Romance 30. They all released eponymous singles during the 80s

THANK YOU!

ACKNOWLEDGEMENTS

Adrian Juste, Alan Read, Andy Kyriacou, Bobby McVay, Brian Nash, Cheryl Baker, Christina Jansen, Christine Staple, Clark Datchler, Dave Wakeling, David Ball, David Brewis, Dennis Seaton, Eddi Reader, Elaine Lane, Heidi Herdman, Ian Donaldson, Jamie Days, James Masterton, Jason Donovan, Jay Aston, Jessica Traetto, John Dredge, Johnny Logan, Jona Lewie, Junior Giscombe, Katherine Charlotte Crawley, Lee MacDonald, Martyn Ware, Matthew Rudd, Mike Nolan, Natalie Owen, Neville Staple, Nick van Eede, Nik Kershaw, Peter Coyle, Richard M. White, Sally-Ann Triplett, Sam Wright, Sarah Moses, Sarah Moss, Tania Hoser, Tanja Surmann

ILLUSTRATIONS

Look Out For Look-in: Champniss
Dear Prudence: Kerry Coltham

Red Rain

Other titles by Sarah Lewis

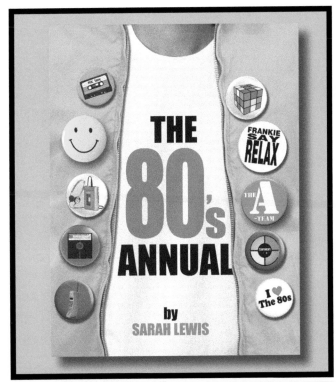

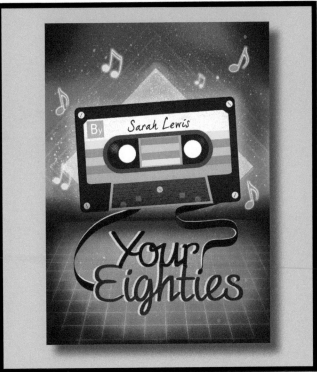

Contact the author:
Website: www.my-eighties.com
Blog: myeighties.wordpress.com
Twitter/Facebook: @MyEighties
Instagram: myeighties

Lightning Source UK Ltd.
Milton Keynes UK
UKHW050855051121
393431UK00002B/42